"When the world screams, 'Do more,' Jesus whispers, 'Trust more.' *Unlimited Motherhood* reminds moms that God desires friendship over performance and that he's not looking for success but obedience. It's these simple acts of faith—which often fly under the radar—that move mountains."

Bob Goff, bestselling author

"The way Jessica Hurlbut weaves storytelling with biblical truth and gentle, kick-in-the-pants encouragement is nothing short of magic. If you've ever had the nagging ache that there was something more for you in life—you're right. *Unlimited Motherhood* will guide you in exploring the radical, unlimited life available only in Jesus."

Becky Keife, author of *No Better Mom for the Job* and other books and Bible studies

"Motherhood is challenging, and we all want to do it well. *Unlimited Motherhood* is a companion gently and humorously pointing us back to the heart of God, which can so easily be forgotten. Thankfully, God is not pushing us to strive and rise to the top. God is waiting for us with wide-open arms to simply be with us in the unseen and seen faithful acts of motherhood."

Tori Hope Petersen, bestselling author of *Fostered*

"A MUST-READ for every mom who's ever stood over the changing table and wondered, *Is* this *what I'm called to?* With humor and conviction, Jessica challenges us to question the limits we've spoken over our lives, then compels us to follow Jesus with everything we have."

Erica Renaud, author of *Pray with Me: Help Your Children Engage in Authentic and Powerful Prayer*, speaker, and former radio host

T0036001

IF I COULD DO ANYTHING FOR GOD

and my time, energy, and resources weren't limited, I would ...

Open a hospital that does not charge the uninsured. —Mackenzie Open a home-less shelter. —Debbie Reform the foster care system. —Olivia Help hospitals create a protocol for our community. —Sandy "Feed" people with his words. —Jaqueline Open a coffeehouse for lonely people. —Minda Travel the USA and evangelize!! —Amy Do missionary trips with family. —Sheri Write, teach, worship with piano. —Tracie Have no child be an orphan. —Shannon Become a missionary family! —Christina Create a camp for kids/youth. —Alison Be more like Mother Teresa. —Marcia I wish I could make the homeless to have homes, the hungry to have food and for people to be nice to each other all the time. —Raeann Own a large family homestead. —Eliza Help hurt women find Jesus. —Michele Build a Christian drug rehab center. —Mary Praise him morn-ing, noon and night! —Denise Go on the mission field. —Jennifer Share the gospel worldwide. —Brittany Help make adaptive equipment more financially accessible. —Sara Teach everyone about HIM. —Laurie Create a healing ministry. —Cindy Give hope to the hopeless. —Taylor Have a camp for kids. —Noree Pray for the sick, lame, blind, oppressed, depressed, posessed, with faith, power, and the authority of Christ and see them set free, healed , mind, body, soul and spirit! I would give God the glory, lead them to Jesus, give them direction to a church, encourage baptism by water and the Holy Spirit! I am already taking steps in that direction and I am seeing it happen! Thank you, Jesus! Finish my first book! Help people who are angry to find peace and happiness through God. —Nicky Raise African children who have no one to care for them. —Laura Elderly care home for all! Worry free! —Nicole Tell the whole world of his un-failing love. —Keeli Ensure every child has a home. —Charity Be more in his presence. —Angela I want to be fearless. —Terry Help bring peace to a chaotic world. —Nicole Have a twelve-bedroom house and foster all the kids I could! —Lila Spread the word of forgiveness! —Denise Build shelters in churches. —Anne Make sure every church has a place for our kids. —Sandy Open a special-needs daycare. —Rebecca Write picture books for kids! —Joy Care for the poor and brokenhearted. —Becky Build a retreat center/camp. —Mary Help all kids to know what it's like to be loved and to love. —Mark Pursue my God-given dream. —Judy Inspire others to be like Jesus. —Elisha Give everyone the power of sight. —Jessica Help single moms. —Kelly Alleviate hunger and homelessness while promoting world peace. —Lori Provide healthcare to the homeless. —Roxanne Build a home for elderly to age with dignity. —Marsha Share his love with everyone. —Melanie Seek to do his will. —Alice Continue to help the homeless. —Lisa Eliminate loneliness. —Cheryl Medical missionary in United States. —Leah Host free meetings where young women could gather to write and share their lives together. Work in developing countries spreading the word and helping underpriviliged children. —*Winter* I would heal hatred so only love remains. Care for children in poverty. —*Emily* Work full-time to end sexual exploitation. —*Joyce* Continue to serve him. Sit at his feet. —*Sara* Do full-time mission work. —*Cindy Anne* Give all humans a home. —*Taylor* Publish VBS curriculum. —*Kayla* I would end abortion. —*Kathleen* Open deluxe boys-and-girls-clubs in small towns. —*Cynthia* Tell souls about Jesus' blood. —*Michelle* Adopt three more children. —*Mary* Go, teach, pray, make disciples. —*Nancy* Help orchestrate a righteous government for God's people! —*Mathia* Work to prevent sexual assaults. —*Destiny* Win a billion souls to Jesus over social media. —*Rebecca* Spend time with him. —*Janneya* Love everyone like Jesus did. —*Dayton* Save the world. —*Victoria* Build the healing center my church dreams of where people can receive emotional healing. —*Angie* Come alongside every broken family. —*Patti* Feed everyone in the world. —*Sarah* Help people to know Jesus and know they are free! —*Carey* Foster and adopt children. —*Kim* Become a faith-based health coach. —*Megan* Open a home for outcasts. —*Monique* Visit children's hospitals with balloons. —*Sarah* Find ways to bring back the feeling of joy in our community so that people would seek it out again in Jesus. —*Renee* Love on kids in Mexico. —*Jennifer* Renovate homes for low-income families. —*Victoria* Open a home—here—for foster children. —*Christie* Open a Christian preschool. —*Patricia* Help women find their value. —*Charity* Use my writing skills more to show God's love! —*Brenda* Support all women who have unplanned pregnancies! —*Diane* Bring the gospel to the lost! —*Christine* Do ministry in New Mexico. —*Mary Ann* Be BOLDER! —*Melanie* Listen with my heart. —*Melanie* Teach unconditional love to everyone. —*Aimee* Produce a Christ-honoring bestselling movie. —*Susan* Complete the Gem Foundation's village in Uganda. —*Tiffany* Travel the world helping women. —*Paula* Take care of medical bills when the families aren't able to and let them know that God loves them. —*Vonda* Lead the world to Christ. —*Alan* Help all those in need. —*Kim* Focus my time on letting others see how great God has made life! —*Justin* Experience the book of Acts. —*Fern* Reach more broken people. —*Nora* Heal the sick and feed the hungry. —*Paulinka* Live intentionally, leaving God-prints everywhere. —*Meredith* Travel the world and tell people about Jesus. —*Racheal* Run a children's home. —*Nikki* Still teach my precious third graders. —*Beth Anne* Serve/bless the sick, poor, and broken. —*Rene* Provide free, staffed disabled housing. —*Annette* Share my testimony with people. —*Jessica* Spread his word further. —*Miya* Help restore abused children. —*Barb* Do kids' ministry full time for special needs families! —*LeeAnn* Grow his kingdom with a nonprofit Christian community center. —*Tammy* Give dying patients a chance to know someone cares about them. —*Bonnie* Heal people by God's power. —*Katariina* Inspire Christian families to adopt. —*Jessica* Feed his sheep. —*Valerie* Create retreats for parent caregivers. —*Kristin Faith* Mentor girls who have had a suicide in their families. —*Glenda* Start a ministry for orphans/displaced youth. —*Alisha*

Unlimited
MOTHERHOOD

*Overcome 12 Limits That Overwhelm
and Conflict Our Hearts*

JESSICA HURLBUT

BETHANYHOUSE
a division of Baker Publishing Group
Minneapolis, Minnesota

Published by Bethany House Publishers
Minneapolis, Minnesota
BethanyHouse.com

Bethany House Publishers is a division of
Baker Publishing Group, Grand Rapids, Michigan

Printed in the United States of America

Library of Congress Cataloging-in-Publication Data
Names: Hurlbut, Jessica, 1982– author.
Title: Unlimited motherhood : overcome 12 limits that overwhelm and conflict our
    hearts / Jessica Hurlbut.
Description: Minneapolis, Minnesota : Bethany House, a division of Baker Publishing
    Group, [2024] | Includes bibliographical references.
Identifiers: LCCN 2023048238 | ISBN 9780764242380 (trade paper) | ISBN
    9780764242809 (casebound) | ISBN 9781493445219 (ebook)
Subjects: LCSH: Motherhood--Religious aspects—Christianity. | Anxiety—Religious
    aspects—Christianity.
Classification: LCC BV4529.18 .H867 2024 | DDC 248.8/431—dc23/eng/20231213
LC record available at https://lccn.loc.gov/2023048238

24   25   26   27   28   29   30   7   6   5   4   3   2   1

For my beautiful daughter Mara.

When life served us bitter water,
the cross of Christ made it oh so sweet.

Discover what's holding you back
from all God has for you.
Take the limits quiz now at
JessicaHurlbut.com.

Contents

Introduction

I hate Christian women's books.

I know that sounds weird coming from a woman who writes Christian books. But I've never been a fan of frilly covers or fluffy messages composed of rhyming words, promising me if I read their book I won't survive, but thrive. It feels like a cheap infomercial, guaranteeing life transformation in thirty days or my money back.

This is *not* that kind of book.

This book is full of gut-wrenching, vulnerable moments coupled with unbelievable God stories of how the Holy Spirit showed up in the middle of my ridiculously limited life.

When I was fifteen, I found a small book tucked away in my grandma's nightstand with a shadowy figure on the cover holding a knife.

Why in the world would Grandma read this?

My grandma spent her days praying the rosary and reading biographies on the lives of the saints, yet here sat a book called *The Cross and the Switchblade.*[1] I couldn't put it down. In one night, I read the entire story of a no-name pastor in the middle of nowhere led by the Holy Spirit to befriend seven teenage gang members on trial in New York City. The rest is history. David Wilkerson's ministry has transformed millions of lives, establishing what is known today as Teen Challenge, a wildly successful Christian addiction program with over 220 centers in the US.[2]

That little book ignited a fire in my heart. I wanted to be a nobody from nowhere who did crazy things for God.

Then life happened.

TO THE MOM WHO HAS DRIFTED
FROM HER FIRST LOVE:

Come home.

1

The White Noise of Distraction

Jesus, cut through the noise

The secret is Christ in me, not me in a different set of circumstances.

—Elisabeth Elliot, *Keep a Quiet Heart*

I'm sure you're familiar with Martin Luther King Jr's civil rights speech, "I Have a Dream."[1] I'd like to present a speech of my own. Give me a second to clear my throat and track down a Pampers box to stand on. It goes like this:

I *had* a dream. (The end.)

Emphasis on the word *had*.

What happened to my dream?

Life.

Maybe you can relate. I could transcribe a mile-long list and I'm sure you could too.

First, I got married—dream diverted.

Then I had kids—dream on hold.

Then my daughter was diagnosed with severe autism—dream obliterated.

Our stories may differ, but I bet you crammed your God dreams in a hall closet too. You know the one I'm talking about: the catch-all closet filled with old yearbooks and the box of DVDs you can't throw away, even though you don't own a DVD player anymore. We can neglect our callings for a season, but every time Jesus cracks open the door, they come spilling out. So what do we do? We become experts at distracting ourselves with trips to the clearance aisles of Target, binge-watching all six seasons of *This Is Us*, and sipping fancy caramel lattes with skim milk and extra whipped cream. At some point, we settle in our mind that we are completely content as a wife and a mom.

I like to lie to myself too.

Yet every once in a while, amid McDonald's Happy Meals and reruns of *Paw Patrol*, I sense a glimmer of hope. A Bible verse awakens my spirit, a memory flashes in my mind, or an ache in my heart cries:

I was made for more.

Now you may argue that my duty as a wife and mom *is* my calling. Guess what?

You win.

My highest calling is my family. My role as a mother and wife is a vocation I don't take lightly and a privilege not all women experience.

Yet when I study women in the New Testament, many were mothers, most were wives, but *all* were disciples. The same commission Jesus gave to the Twelve he proclaimed to the crowds of women following him: "Go and make disciples of all nations" (Matthew 28:19).

The Great Commission keeps me up at night.

How do we make disciples if the circumstances of life are holding us hostage? How do we shine the light of Christ if we struggle to leave the four walls of our house? How in a season jam-packed with limits do we go into all the world, when most days we can't find time to go to the bathroom?

I transitioned from working full-time, to part-time, to no-time due to the severe behaviors of my daughter on the spectrum. For eight years, I was unable to go to church, stores, restaurants, or even make it through a drive-thru because of my daughter's aggressive meltdowns.

I *understand* limits.

Yet when I complain to God, he reminds me of the apostle Paul. Paul wrote much of the New Testament while in prison. I'm not comparing my home to a jail cell. It's more like house arrest. It's as if someone strapped a tracker to my ankle and when I venture fifty feet from my yard, it screams, "Mom!" Yet Paul established and pastored the early church. His life and words are still transforming the Christian world as we know it. Somehow the Holy Spirit who resided in Paul was not limited by the confines of his life.

The same is true for you.

In his letter to the Church of Ephesus, Paul, held captive in a Roman prison, penned these powerful words:

> Now all glory to God, who is able, through his mighty power at work within us, to accomplish infinitely more than we might ask or think.
>
> Ephesians 3:20 NLT

Is Paul the exception to the rule? Do you believe God and his *mighty power at work in you* can accomplish infinitely more than you could ask or think?

He can.

He will.

If you allow him.

To all who feel shackled by their current state of affairs, there's hope.

Why?

With God, all ceilings are man-made.

Rooftop Revelation

"Jess, come see." Glenroy seized my arm as we passed in the hallway.

"See what?"

We were volunteering at a Christian school in Queens as part of our urban ministry assignment, but I assumed my friend wanted to play hooky and I was game.

I swung my hip against the crash bar, throwing open the metal door as the cool breeze rushed in. Gravel crinkled beneath our feet, scaring our onlookers—the pigeons—away. The typical blue-gray city skyline was filled with clouds of billowing smoke.

"Is a building on fire?"

"A plane hit the World Trade Center," Glenroy said.

I strained to see through the haze the outline of hundreds of people running toward Upper Manhattan. The mass exodus petrified me more than the smoke and fire pouring out of the tower. The stench of burned rubber wafted into my nostrils, causing my stomach to churn. This much was clear: the United States was under attack. I wasn't viewing this atrocity safely through the glass of a TV screen. I was a character smack-dab in the middle of history.

I stuffed my shaking hands into my pockets and returned to the classroom. Our mentor teacher instructed us not to panic. Our lesson plans would remain unchanged. No recess. No exiting the building. The teacher ordered us to pretend as if everything was fine while the world outside our door was crumbling.

> Life is too short and people are too precious to waste time being Christians who talk a lot but do very little.

Parents trickled into the school, having hiked miles from their offices in Lower Manhattan. They resembled living shadows, gray ash caked on their hair and bodies. The only color shining through was the whites of their eyes. Panic-stricken, they harassed the secretary, demanding to pull their kids out of school. Our classroom size dwindled, and by the end of the day, only fifty students remained. As college interns, we oversaw the after-school program. I leaned against a metal water fountain as the magnitude of the day sunk in. As I watched a handful of carefree kids run around the gym dodging nerf balls, I couldn't help but wonder if any of them would ever see their parents again.

An Instant Message from Jesus

This three-month internship in New York City was the jump scare my spirit needed. I don't know when it happened, but at some point I swapped my first love for polite manners, devotional readings, and sporadic church attendance. None of these things are wrong, but they don't equate to a living, breathing, dynamic relationship with Jesus. But after 9-11, I grew desperate for God to use me. Life is too short and people are too precious to waste time being Christians who talk a lot but *do* very little.

I had invested two years in Bible college studying God's Word. But attending Bible college is like living in an alternate universe. Everyone is happy. Everyone loves Jesus. Everyone debates theology, drinks lattes, and utilizes side hugs. But whenever I returned home on break, the reality of a broken world slapped me in the face. One Christmas, a good friend confessed to me she was raped. I had no advice to offer. I threw up a quick prayer and scooted out the door.

I lay in bed later that night ashamed of myself.

How can I be a youth pastor if I can't even help a close friend?

I continued complaining until a God thought interrupted my pity party:

"Just do what I tell you to do."

I'll try, Jesus.

I rolled over and drifted off to sleep with a sliver of peace and a massive headache.

The next day, while playing a game of solitaire on my computer, I felt God prod me to reach out to an old friend from high school and send him an instant message.

Now this is getting weird, Jesus.

I turned on worship music and paced my bedroom.

I spent twenty minutes arguing with God. Finally, I mustered up the nerve to click on Greg's name as the bridge of a Jason Upton song swelled in the background. Tears splashed onto my keyboard as I typed out a line from the worship song and reluctantly hit send: "Run, run, run away from me, you'll end up running right into me."[2]—Jesus.

Frantic, I signed off for fear he would respond. I vowed to spend the next two days living as a hermit, afraid to bump into Greg in our small town. After the initial rush of adrenaline faded, a strange peace overwhelmed me.

I had obeyed.

I listened to God's voice and actually followed through.

I had never experienced this sensation before. Jesus refers to this sentiment in the Gospels as spiritual food. Concerned with Jesus' physical well-being, the disciples pleaded with him to eat something. His response?

I have food to eat that you know nothing about.

John 4:32

Jesus' friends assumed he must have a secret stash. Like the bag of M&M's hidden in your underwear drawer which only emerge at the end of the night when your kids are fast asleep. Yet Jesus wasn't talking about literal food. He was referring to a fullness in our souls which only occurs when we hear God's voice and obey.

I never believed my words could change a life. They are merely letters on a page without the breath of the Holy Spirit. But one word typed in obedience can move mountains. Little did I know that my message would reach Greg at one of the darkest times of his life.

Alonebutnotforsaken

Greg slipped his hand under his pillowcase and felt for the metal bottle opener. Cracking a Molson Canadian, he stared out the frost-covered window of his dorm room.

Heading north to spend Christmas with family, Greg looked forward to reconnecting with old friends. But a week later, at a New Year's Eve party, things felt different. The alcohol wasn't working. Painful memories broke through the surface, taunting him like the Whac-a-Mole game at the arcade. Each beer, a swing of his rubber mallet, crushed one only to have another pop up in its place.

Greg scanned the room. The drunken behavior around him sounded like the screeching of a fork across a dinner plate and something in him snapped. Like King Solomon, he envisioned himself screaming at the top of his lungs, "Vanity! Vanity! All is vanity!" Instead, he climbed onto a nearby coffee table, lifted his arms with a red SOLO cup in hand, and declared, "What are we doin' here?" Pointing his finger at the people around the room, he yelled, "None of it—none of this matters!"

After Greg delivered his eloquent speech, a few awkward chuckles followed. He lost his balance and slipped backward off the coffee table. The brown-and-orange checkered couch in his buddy's basement broke his fall. He chugged a few more beers and blacked out.

When he returned home the next morning, an emptiness clung to Greg. His life felt like a cheap Walmart bag. Each day, he would browse the aisles with a plastic sack draped over his arm.

Hmm, what else can I put in here?

His flimsy bag was chock-full of possessions and distractions: a successful sound business, friends, a truck, money, alcohol, ski trips to Titus Mountain. Yet we all know those dang Walmart bags tear so easily. Greg discovered the distractions of life were empty promises, as his possessions slipped out of his plastic bag and crashed onto the blacktop of the parking lot.

What is one more thing I can add to my life to make me happy?

For five hours, Greg tried to answer this question while lying in bed.

Nothing.

It doesn't matter *what* you add if there is a hole in your bag.

An all-or-nothing type of guy—Greg felt his life was no longer worth living. He snuck downstairs with one goal: to drive his truck as fast as the speedometer would allow and let go of the wheel. As he reached for the doorknob, a strange thought popped into his head.

I should check my instant messages. Maybe someone from the party is worried about me.

He snuck into his dad's office, logged onto the computer, and found not a single message from his maxed-out buddy list. But one message flashed from a username he did not recognize: *Alonebut-notforsaken*. As he slid the cursor over the accept button, these words popped up on his screen: "Run, run, run away from me, you'll end up running right into me."—Jesus

Greg doubled over as this truth shot through his heart: *God is the one thing.*

Staggering to the office door, he slammed it.

"Honey?" A light knock came from outside. "Are you okay?" His mom pressed her ear against the wall and strained to hear the commotion inside.

His tears morphed into sobs as a whirlwind of questions thrashed within Greg's mind. He couldn't make sense of this divine moment. Not a soul knew of his plan to commit suicide. Yet he sat and stared at a computer screen, mesmerized by this life-saving text.

God sees me.

God hears me.

God knows me.

And the same is true for you.

God sees you.

God hears you.

God knows you.

God's thoughts toward you are more than all the grains of sand in the ocean. Have you ever tried to scoop a handful of sand and count each granule? It's impossible. God never stops thinking about you. And what's more unbelievable? If you tune your ear and listen, he desires to use *you* to convey one tiny granule of love to someone in need.

White Noise

You might be wondering, *How do I hear God's voice?*

This, my friend, is the million-dollar question. But before I explain, let's talk about the reason why we *don't* hear God. I call it the white noise of distraction.

Who doesn't love sleep? I vote moms should hibernate for half the year. When it comes to sleeping, my husband can't get a good night's rest without a fan. (While traveling, he once tried to fit one in his carry-on suitcase.) The white noise a fan creates masks other sounds, helping us sleep better. Unfortunately, the enemy utilizes white noise in our lives too. How? In the form of everyday distractions. If pain is God's wake-up call, distractions are the white noise which lulls us back to sleep.

As moms, we have more distractions than Baby Shark has views on YouTube. We have bums to wipe, bills to pay, breakfast to fry, and beds to make—to name a few. And those are outward distractions. We're also experts in allowing the enemy to plague our minds with inward diversions. We worry about our kids' futures, our growing waistlines, our finances, other people's opinions, and our husband's stress levels. You get the idea. Distractions are the lullabies the enemy sings as we doze off. Then he creeps toward us with a pillow to muffle the voice of our Father.

If pain is God's wake-up call, distractions are the white noise which lulls us back to sleep.

Jesus once told a story about a farmer scattering seeds. Some of the seeds fell on the path and the birds gobbled them up. Others landed on rocky ground and did not take root. But some seeds found their home in fertile soil, only for thorns to choke the life out of them. The thorns represent the cares of this world. In short, thorns suffocate (Matthew 13:1–23).

Suffocating.

Isn't this how life feels sometimes? In one of his comedy routines, Jim Gaffigan tells the audience, "If you wanna know what it's like to have a fourth kid, just imagine you're drowning and then someone hands you a baby."[3] I burst out in laughter and tears simultaneously. For moms, every day feels like we are treading water with our noses barely above the surface.

When my children were younger, I never stopped changing diapers and pulling Cheerios from between my toes. Now that my kids are older, I'm a glorified Uber driver. The distractions never stop—they change. We will never have free time to seek God. We must *intentionally* pursue it.

Quiet Minds

So how do we combat a world full of distractions? The answer is a five-letter word: Q-U-I-E-T. As moms, if we discover a free moment, we tend to doze off within the first thirty seconds. I fall asleep at red lights. (I should be diagnosed with narcolepsy, but I don't have time for that.) And some days, the only time I find to pray is while running the vacuum cleaner. (It drowns out the screams of the children. You should try it.) For a busy mom, it's less about having a *quiet time* and more about having a *quiet mind*.

When we think Jesus only speaks to the Proverbs 31 woman who rises with the sun and studies twenty-five chapters of the Bible, we disqualify ourselves. If we hold tight to these fables, the enemy wins. Throw in a whole gamut of distractions to keep our thoughts racing and our hands busy, and our defeat is imminent.

God's voice isn't a secret treasure few discover but rather an accessible relationship available to all.

Here's the trouble: God is always speaking. But our hearing is intermittent. God's voice is like a radio signal. Just as a transmitter sends electromagnetic signals over long distances, God is broadcasting his thoughts, directions, and truth to anyone who will listen. Throughout the New Testament we see the phrase, "Whoever has ears, let them hear."[4] We are the receiver, the device which picks up the radio signal. Yet most of us wander around clueless of the signals traveling above our heads. We only hear silence when we pray because our ears aren't tuned in to the right frequency.

Determined to hear God's voice, I implemented a daily practice. Each morning, I sit before God with a folded piece of paper. On the left-hand side of the page, I write *My Thoughts*. Below this heading, I scribble my concerns, worries, and requests. On the right-hand side of the page, I write *God's Thoughts*. Setting the pen down, I pray: Jesus, what is *one thing* you want me to do today? Not ten things, not a five-year plan, not a Bible verse, or a word for the year. Just one thing. I spend five minutes listening. I never hear a booming voice, but I often receive a passing thought.

Call your friend Sarah, she's struggling.

Make banana bread and deliver it to the neighbor.

Pull the Legos out and spend the day crawling on the floor with your babies.

It doesn't sound grand. Oftentimes, it feels random. On most occasions, I think I made it up. But if I step out in faith and do whatever *it* is, God shows up in a powerful way.

Sheep from Goats

The one who enters by the gate is the shepherd of the sheep. The gatekeeper opens the gate for him, and the sheep *listen to his voice*. He calls his own sheep by name and leads them out. When he has brought out all his own, he goes on ahead of them, and his sheep follow him because they *know his voice.* But they will never follow a stranger; in fact, they will run away from him because they do not recognize a stranger's voice.

John 10:2–5, italics added

I never understood this verse until I watched videos of shepherds interacting with their sheep. Take a break and head over to YouTube and search "shepherds calling their sheep." You'll find several clips where people other than the shepherd attempt to call the sheep. The sheep won't budge. When a stranger comes too close, the sheep run away. But the most beautiful sight is when the shepherd calls the sheep to himself. (Grab some tissues.) The flock comes running and gathers around their master in a matter of minutes.[5]

In Matthew 25, Jesus describes himself as the Good Shepherd, and the scene is Judgment Day. With all the people of the earth standing before him, Jesus does something rather odd:

All the nations will be gathered before him, and he will separate the people one from another as a shepherd separates the sheep from the goats.

Matthew 25:32

The sheep symbolize those who know Christ, while the goats represent the stubborn ones who prefer to go their own way. But how would a shepherd manage to separate these two animals? *His voice.* During the day, the shepherds in Palestine often allow sheep and goats to mingle in the same field. But at night, he separates these two animals with a unique call. The hard-headed, independent goats ignore the call. But the sheep come running.

I pray your heart's desire is to hear God's voice and follow his lead. But how do we master this skill?

Trial and error.

I'm pretty sure you don't like this answer. We want to know *for sure* God is directing us to do something. Yet if we're certain, we would be removing faith from the equation. And the Bible says it is *impossible* to please God without faith.[6] God isn't pleased by our polite manners, our well-behaved children, our charitable donations, or our church attendance. God is pleased by our faith.

> God isn't pleased by our polite manners, our well-behaved children, our charitable donations, or our church attendance. God is pleased by our faith.

Six months after Greg's God encounter, he left the state school he attended and enrolled in the Christian college where I was studying.

You have no idea the power of God within you.

Power to change a life.

Power to write the most amazing stories of redemption.

All you have to do is hand over the pen to an Author far better than you.

PRAY THIS: *Dear Jesus, I'm sorry for ignoring you. Forgive me for drifting from my first love and allowing myself to be distracted by the noise of this world. I want to learn to follow your lead. Don't allow me to be satisfied living as a status-quo Christian. Help me tune in to your voice and step out in faith, even when I'm scared out of my mind. Amen.*

DO THIS: Buy a prayer journal or a simple notebook will do. Each morning set aside ten minutes and draw a line down the center of the page. Label the left side of the paper *My Thoughts* and the right side *God's Thoughts*. Share your concerns with God and then set down the pen and ask God what *one* thing he wants you to do today. Really listen. When a thought pops into your mind, don't doubt it. Write it down and make this task your top priority. Then watch what God can do with one tiny step of obedience.

TO THE MOM WHO ALLOWS FEAR TO HOLD HER BACK:

Jesus is on the other side of this paper-thin wall— waiting. Fear isn't a force field keeping you from Jesus, but a flimsy lie that tears when you take one step toward him.

2

The Friction of Fear

Jesus, keep me moving

Fear is a self-imposed prison that will keep you from becoming
what God intends for you to be.

—Rick Warren, *The Purpose Driven Life*

When God shows up in outrageous ways, it's easy to hand over
our pen and allow him to write our story. The fog clears and we
see God for who he is—an amazing Father with a perfect plan.
Yet the minute things go dark and we hit a pothole, we snatch
that dang pen out of his hand. Jarred back to reality with another
negative pregnancy test, a call from the ICU, or divorce papers
in our mailbox.

I can write this story better, Jesus.

No matter how many God moments I experience, the next
time I'm faced with a big decision, I'm derailed by fear. Fear slows
us down, pulls us over, and robs us of our destiny. Fear loves to
steal stuff.

The list of things you're afraid of may be longer than your weekly grocery store receipt. As a mom, I worry less about *my* future and more about *my kids'* future. Will they go to the right college? Will they marry someone I approve of? Will they love Jesus? Don't even get me started on the state of this fallen world. If the economy is bad now, how much worse will it be in twenty years? If inflation is high, what will gas prices look like in the future? If morality is taking a nose dive, what kind of world will my grandbabies grow up in? How will their faith survive?

Fear slows us down, pulls us over, and robs us of our destiny. Fear loves to steal stuff.

If we're honest, we don't have a fear issue, but a trust issue. For some reason, it's far easier to admit we're afraid than to confess:

"I don't trust you, God."

But you don't.

And neither did I.

The Honest Confession

Greg and I stood below the glow of the floodlights outside the girls' dorm room. We swatted mosquitoes as we chatted about the shenanigans of the day. Although we were childhood friends, I now looked up to Greg—literally and spiritually. He was sold out for God, and I relished the fact that somebody got me. We skipped church on Sundays to devote time to people in the city. This led to some wild adventures. Today's escapade consisted of praying for a homeless man, cramming all three of us in his pickup, and hearing the man's life story over beef baja chalupas.

While hanging outside my dorm, our conversation shifted to the future.

"I've no clue what I want to do with my life. I just want to do what God wants," Greg said.

"It's hard for me to think about the future," I admitted while twisting the promise ring my parents gave me when I turned sixteen around my finger. "I picture myself as an old maid living alone, working in a library, like Mary in the movie *It's a Wonderful Life.*"

"Are you kidding me? You're going to find Mr. Right, have a bunch of kids, and do great things for God," Greg said.

"Well, it's not a matter of finding someone," I said as I stared at the ground, kicking gravel with my feet. "It's a matter of trusting someone, and I never will."

> But just because you love someone, doesn't mean you trust them.

I wanted to suck the words back into my mouth. I glanced at Greg, only to discover his eyes welling with tears.

"Why are *you* crying? I should be the one crying," I said, trying to keep it together.

"That's the saddest thing I've ever heard. You're the most amazing person I know. To think you'd choose to be alone. It's so sad."

At that moment, I fell in love.

But just because you love someone, doesn't mean you trust them.

Fear Makes Us Hide

I didn't always have trust issues. My wounds from past betrayals festered into open sores. They hurt too much, so I didn't want anyone to touch them. I never allowed Jesus to come close enough to slather on Neosporin and bandage me up. When others fail us, we struggle to get back on our feet. When it seems God has failed us, oftentimes, we never recover. I loved God—but man—I didn't trust him one bit. I put more stock in Amazon delivering my package in two days than I did in God's faithfulness.

Our conflict with fear and trust stems back to the beginning.

In the Garden of Eden, Adam and Eve had it made. They spent their days sunbathing in paradise and counting their steps on nightly strolls with the Creator of the Universe. Everything they wanted or needed was at their fingertips. Everything except the fruit from one tree: the Tree of the Knowledge of Good and Evil. This one tree God instructed them not to snack on. Yet Adam and Eve couldn't resist.

> Then the man and his wife heard the sound of the Lord God as he was walking in the garden in the cool of the day, and they hid from the Lord God among the trees of the garden. But the Lord God called to the man, "Where are you?"
>
> Genesis 3:8–9

Adam and Eve hijacked the pen from God's hand and decided they would determine what was right and wrong. They placed their trust in themselves rather than in their Creator. And don't we do the same thing? How often do we rush to make a decision without spending time in prayer? How much energy do we waste weighing the pros and cons while neglecting to ask God's opinion? Our decisions are sacred, and if we have surrendered our lives to Jesus, he should have a say in every one. Taking matters into their own hands was Adam and Eve's downfall, and it's ours too.

We are doomed to repeat this cycle of sin, shame, and hiding. Hyperaware of our imperfections, we tend to push God and people away. And if we hide for too long, we discover a terrible truth: people stop looking. Thankfully, God never does. When he asked, "Adam, where are you?" God knew his exact GPS location. He knows right where we are. Rather, he asks this question so we can come to the realization he has never left us. *We* are the ones hiding, while God has been there all along.

Trust Is Risky Business

We sped down the highway with the windows cranked in Greg's 1988 Chevy pickup. The wind whipped through my hair and into my eyes and mouth. A faded green Christmas tree air freshener dangled from the rearview mirror. It was a failed attempt to cover up the overpowering stench of petroleum. There was a hole in the oil pan, causing us to pull over every hundred miles. Each stop required Greg to buy another quart of oil and refill the tank to prevent the engine from seizing.

I guess we liked to live on the wild, broke, and slightly irresponsible side. Headed back to college after a youth conference in Virginia, we were reeling after all God had done.

Without giving it a second thought, I reached across the bench seat and grabbed Greg's hand. He snapped his head to the side and stared at me with a wild look in his eyes. He slowly turned back toward the road, and we drove in silence until we pulled over for our routine oil stop. Five minutes later, Greg climbed back into the truck, reeking like a mechanic.

"I don't hold hands with friends. Do you?" Greg asked with a scowl on his face.

I shook my head.

"I'm not sure what this is, but I don't date girls for fun. If I'm going to date someone, I'm all in. Is this serious?"

I nodded.

And then—like the instance in front of the girls' dorm—Greg teared up as words spewed out of his mouth like a broken fire hydrant:

"I love you. I love you. I love you. I love you. I love you. I love you."

The more he repeated himself, the harder I shook my head. Tears trickled down my face as a spirit of rejection rose up within me. Greg inched closer as I pushed his shoulders away.

"I love you. I love you. I love you. I love you. I love you. I love you."

This phrase washed over my soul like the tide, exposing a secret I buried in the sand for years—I didn't know how to receive love.

Love without a Hook in It

As a young adult, whenever I sensed rejection, I would run to the bathroom and stick my finger down my throat. I wasn't bulimic or anorexic. But I was desperate to rid myself of myself. Self-hate will make you do the most bizarre things.

For years, I searched for help, devouring books on self-care. But they never seemed to make a difference. I felt like I was back in elementary school, cranking an old-school pencil sharpener to get my life on point. Yet I continually pulled out broken lead. Because loving yourself isn't something you can work toward—it's something you receive.

I found myself overwhelmed with anger the day Greg professed his love. Love makes you furious when you feel you don't deserve it. But after the hundredth time, something in me broke. God leans in and whispers those same words to you over and over again. Self-help books will never solve your problems. We must learn to receive the perfect love of the Father.

> There is no fear in love. But perfect love drives out fear.
>
> 1 John 4:18

The Greek word for *fear* in this passage means to put to flight. Something about fear makes us want to run the other way. Why? Because we're petrified the person on the opposite side of the equation will discover how messed up we are.

For years, I had it backward. I was convinced I needed to look like Barbie, be the valedictorian, eat all my vegetables, and never screw up to earn God's love. We aren't meant to waste our lives striving for perfection. We simply receive Christ's perfect love. Perfection was never required of us. Jesus has that base covered.

And the beauty of God's love is that he is faithful when we are not. His love is constant. Never wavering. Never diminishing. Never changing its mind. The Greek word for God's love is *agape,* love without a hook in it. Unlike human love—filled with angles, motives, and self-serving agendas—God's love gives and never expects anything in return. When his love comes, fear must go.

> There is no need to run when you're loved completely. Love that never changes its mind kicks our need to run to the curb.
>
> 1 John 4:18 Hurlbut Translation

Let your guard down. Permit God to touch the painful wounds you've been hiding. Allow his perfect love to come rushing in. And watch in amazement as the dam of fear which held you back for years crumbles at your feet.

As I grew more secure in his perfect love, I felt God calling me to not only trust his *heart* but to follow his *lead*.

Angels Browsing Books-A-Million

As I swung open the fingerprinted glass door, the smell of fresh ground espresso came wafting out. My roommate, Greg, and I were killing time at a local bookstore, browsing the shelves before we headed to the movies.

A young man with a warm smile and floppy hair bounced by us sporting a hoodie from the college we attended. As he exited the store, he spun around and asked, "Do you guys attend Southeastern?"

"Yeah," I said.

"Cool. I went there for a couple of years until God asked me to drop everything and move to Africa," the stranger explained. "I'm a missionary, but I'm spending a few months in the states."

We smiled and nodded, assuming he was on his way out. Instead, he turned his gaze toward me and asked a strange question.

"Would you quit college if God asked you to?"

I glanced at my friends, raised my eyebrows, and shrugged my shoulders.

He continued, "Sometimes, our refusal to let go of good things robs us of God's best."

And just as he had mysteriously appeared, the man strolled away midsentence, mumbling something about seeing us in heaven one day.

Whenever I look back on this moment, I can't help but wonder if he was a real person or an angel. Little did I know, this five-minute encounter with a stranger would change the trajectory of my life.

College Dropouts

"I think God wants me to move home," I said, biting my lip as we headed out of the movie theater.

"Move home? You only have one semester left. Is this because of the weird guy at the bookstore?" Greg asked.

"I don't know. Maybe. I need to pray about it."

The Books-A-Million incident was messing with my head. I couldn't answer yes to the question the stranger proposed. It didn't make sense. Why would God lead me to Florida to pursue a degree but not complete it? Yet a part of me knew I was cramming God into my neat four-year education box. I was expecting him to submit to *my* logical plan rather than *his* mysterious one.

A few days later, I found myself at a chapel service and I felt compelled to read Ezekiel chapter 3. As I read, a verse leaped off the page:

> Then the Spirit entered me and put me on my feet. He said, "Go home and shut the door behind you."
>
> Ezekiel 3:24 THE MESSAGE

I don't recommend playing Bible roulette. Bible roulette is when you close your eyes, open your Bible to a random page, and point to a verse to hear from God. The Bible isn't a magic eight ball. But this was not my intent. In the midst of worship, the Holy Spirit impressed this chapter on my heart. Was this a confirmation that I should pack my bags and head home, or was I reading into everything? One thing was for sure: the idea of moving home terrified me.

Cheerleaders on the Side of the Highway

Friction is a force that works against the forward motion of an object. Fear is the Great Resistance. Anxiety, worry, and fear grind our momentum in the things of God to a halt.

Maybe you've been there. Have you ever sensed God calling you to do something but a few days later you talked yourself out of it? You felt compelled to start a ministry. But when you surveyed the demands on your life as a mom, you concluded it wasn't realistic. God stirred your family's heart to take a leap of faith and move. But after several late-night conversations, you changed your mind. A sermon challenged you to consider fostering a child, but the what-ifs tormented you, so you shelved the idea. God asked you to create deeper friendships with women in your church. But you found yourself unable to initiate a conversation. We may know where we need to go, but the friction of fear prevents us from making our next move.

I tend to run out of gas. Not the exhaustion at the end of a long day; I mean gasoline. I'm notorious for not checking the gas gauge, and it is my husband's pet peeve. Do you know the last thing I need when my gas tank is on E? A pep talk. Imagine a whole squad of cheerleaders lined up along the sides of the highway I'm stranded on chanting:

"Give me a J!"

"J!"

"You've got your J, you've got your J."

"Give me an E!"

"E!"

"You've got your E, you've got your E."

Although their cheering would be entertaining, it would get me nowhere. Why do we assume fear can be conquered through a glorified pep talk? Pastors declare from the pulpit, "Do it afraid." We decorate our living room with Hobby Lobby plaques that state *Faith Over Fear*. We sound like a bunch of high school cheerleaders waving our pompoms. If overcoming fear was that simple, we'd all be experiencing the all-my-poker-chips-are-in-the-center-of-the-table life God has called us to.

But we're not.

Because fear isn't something we can talk ourselves out of—stepping out in faith is.

The Great Wall of Surrender

A few days passed, and the thought of quitting college persisted like a leaky faucet. I overanalyzed everything, annoying my roommate to no end. It got to the point where she wondered if she should move home too. One afternoon, while all three of us were munching on yogurt-covered pretzels in the college café, Greg said something strange:

"Following Jesus is like a giant trust fall—either he catches you or he doesn't—a daring act of faith."

I perked up, pushed my chair back, and stood to my feet, "That's it. Let's do it."

"Do what?" they responded in unison.

"Let's find the highest height on campus and jump off. It will be a symbolic act of surrendering our lives to God."

"I'm in," Greg said while laughing at the absurdity of what we were about to do.

"You two are unbelievable," my roommate countered.

But with some positive peer pressure, my roommate caved. An hour later, all three of us found ourselves perched on top of the tallest staircase on campus with our legs dangling over the side.

"It doesn't look too far down," I lied to make everyone feel better.

Without a warning, Greg sprang from the ledge, hit the ground, and rolled onto the grass.

"It's further than it looks," he yelled up with his hands cupped around his mouth.

I was next. After ten minutes and a few false starts, I hung off the ledge by my fingertips. My knees scrapped across the beige stucco wall.

> The Holy Spirit is the secret sauce to the Christian life.

"Close your eyes and just let go," Greg hollered. *Here goes nothing, Jesus.*

I released my hands and dropped with a thud, rolling my ankle.

We laughed and joked about this moment all night. And as foolish as it was, I felt different. Fear's chokehold loosened and I knew it was time to move home.

Do It Filled

If fear is the Great Resistance, how do we find courage to push past it? Knowing God loves you is not enough. Think about the disciples. They were fully aware of Christ's love. John often bragged he was Jesus' favorite. Yet after the crucifixion, what did they do? They hid in the upper room.

> On the evening of that first day of the week, when the disciples were together, with the doors locked for fear of the Jewish leaders, Jesus came and stood among them and said, "Peace be with you!"
>
> John 20:19

Jesus met the disciples *in their fear.* Jesus didn't expect his followers to muster up the courage to save the world. Instead, he came to them in their fear and comforted them with his peace. To the doubters, he gave permission to touch the wounds in his hands and side. He didn't instruct them to kick fear in the teeth. And a week later, when the disciples were hiding again, he repeated the process. Jesus never even addressed their fear. Instead, he did something radically different:

> And with that he breathed on them and said, "Receive the Holy Spirit."
>
> John 20:22

The Holy Spirit is the secret sauce to the Christian life. We will never be able to conquer fear without the third person of the Trinity. After the resurrection, Jesus appeared to the disciples on and off for forty days. At his last meal with his friends, he gave some bizarre instructions. He advised the disciples to *return* to the upper room—back to the space where they were hiding in the first place.

> "Do not leave Jerusalem, but wait for the gift my Father promised, which you have heard me speak about. For John baptized with water, but in a few days you will be baptized with the Holy Spirit." . . . Then the apostles returned to Jerusalem. . . . They went upstairs to the room where they were staying. . . . They all joined together constantly in prayer.
>
> Acts 1:4–5, 12–14

Isn't it strange Jesus didn't say, "Get over your fears, you big babies?" Instead, he told them to return to the little room where they were hiding.

He knew the disciples didn't have what it takes and neither do we.

Jesus asked his friends to pray and wait for the Holy Spirit. Without the Holy Spirit, our lives will be lame. We will hide away in our little homes with our little families and our little routines until Jesus returns. We desperately need the power of the Spirit to bust through the paper-thin wall of fear that is holding us back. Jesus didn't say, "Do it afraid." He said, "Do it filled."

More Than an Imaginary Friend

To understand why we need the Spirit, let's back up a bit. Right before Jesus went to the cross, he said, "It is best for you that I go away . . ." (John 16:7 NLT).

Can you imagine spending three years with Jesus face-to-face? Witnessing limbs grow out, blind eyes opened, and corpses coming back to life. Until Jesus looks at you one day and says, "I should leave. You'd be better off if I wasn't around."

Why would Jesus make such an outlandish statement?

He understood something we don't. Jesus didn't view the Holy Spirit as an imaginary friend void of power but as the essential third person of the Godhead. In the Old Testament, because of mankind's sinful state, the Spirit only rested upon someone for a brief moment. But through Jesus' death and resurrection, he can now settle in and make his home in us. All we have to do is ask.

> I tell you the truth, anyone who believes in me will do the same works I have done, and even greater works, because I am going to be with the Father.
>
> John 14:12 NLT

I always wondered how we could top Jesus in the miracle department. How could a stay-at-home special needs mom perform *greater works*? But take a look at the second half of this verse. Jesus explained the reason we will do greater works is because he is going to be with his Father.

And who comes when Jesus leaves?

The Holy Spirit.

It's simple math:

Jesus living on the earth filled with the Spirit = 1 Jesus.

Every believer on the earth filled with the Spirit = 2.6 billion miniature versions of Jesus.[1]

The early church resembled Jesus so much that they acquired the nickname "little Christs." This is where we get the word *Christian*. May we be miniature versions of Jesus wherever we go as we continue to witness firsthand the multiplication effect of his kingdom.

Go Home and Shut the Door Behind You

"I'm moving home at the end of the semester," I said while walking toward the college cafeteria for dinner. Greg didn't act surprised. He sensed it the day I hung off the ledge of our college staircase.

"I'm coming with you," Greg said.

"Are you sure? Don't do this because of me."

"I'm not. Trust me," Greg replied.

And for the first time, I did.

So we hit the road in his oil-leaking, gas-guzzling pickup and drove 1,500 miles north with no money, no plans—just blind faith—because in the end, that's all you really need.

PRAY THIS: *Dear Holy Spirit, I desperately need you but you kind of scare me. Help me to let go of control and surrender the pen of my life to you. I know without you, I can't be all God has created me to be. Comfort me when I'm afraid. Guide me into truth. Give me wisdom and boldness to step out in faith. Empower me to live the life God designed for me before the world began.*

DO THIS: After praying this prayer, turn on some worship music and linger a bit. Just as Jesus told the disciples to wait, we should not be in a hurry. Invite the Holy Spirit to come into your life. You may feel goosebumps or a sense of peace. This is the tangible presence of God, the Holy Spirit. Let him speak to you, fill you, and comfort you. If you cry, let the tears flow. He wants to heal deep places in your heart you didn't even know existed.

TO THE MOM WHO HIDES IN THE BACKGROUND:

You matter.

Your life has purpose.

Your words have power.

It's time to step out from the shadows and open your mouth.

3

The Shush of Silence

Jesus, open my mouth

The fact that I am a woman does not make me a different kind of Christian, but the fact that I am a Christian does make me a different kind of woman.

—Elisabeth Elliot, *Let Me Be a Woman*

I ugly cried the morning after my wedding.

The flowers were perfect. The ceremony, flawless. The groom, my best friend. But I woke the next day with the same gnawing ache in my heart.

I. Still. Feel. Alone.

Greg and I found ourselves at the altar eight months after we moved home. I was twitterpated. When Greg's name flashed on my caller ID, my stomach felt like one of those fidget spinners. Yet the day after our vows, the void remained. I found Mr. Right, yet the pain persisted. I learned the hard way that no person on earth can fill an ache created for eternity.

Hallmark movies and, dare I say it, Christian culture spoon-feeds us a lie we're gobbling up: marriage is the goal. Teen girls waste years fantasizing about their Instagram-worthy weddings. Twentysomethings daydream of the moment they meet the one—the missing puzzle piece that will snap into place. Yet God created marriage to be like a tag-team wrestling match. Two become one so we can chokehold the devil faster. Two become one so we can pace each other side-by-side as we chase after the things of God. Two become one to accomplish exponentially more for the kingdom than we could alone. Our desire for someone to complete us can never be met in a relationship on this side of heaven.

> **God created marriage to be like a tag-team wrestling match.**

The apostle Paul said it best:

> Now I know in part; then I shall know fully, even as I am fully known.
>
> 1 Corinthians 13:12

To be loved by someone who doesn't know us is a skin-deep-Tinder relationship. To be fully known by someone and rejected is our worst nightmare. But to be fully known and completely loved is a gift only God the Father can give.

I've never confessed to anyone—including my husband—that I cried the morning after our wedding. But like Jesus' mother Mary, as women, we are really good at keeping quiet and storing all these things in our hearts.

Bridal College

A cold draft seeped through the leaded glass window of my dorm room. I climbed up to my bed and wrapped a fleece blanket around my shoulders. I leafed through the college orientation packet. After ten minutes of awkward silence, I hung my head upside down to chat with my roommate on the bunk below.

"What are you studying? I'm in the youth ministry tract."

"I don't know. I just wanna marry a cute boy who loves Jesus. There is a reason they call Bible college, bridal college," my roommate said.

I jerked my head upward to roll my eyes without an audience. Over the next few weeks, this conversation occurred repeatedly. Cathy wanted to be a pastor's wife. Shelly dreamed of marrying a missionary. Monica hoped to find a good man, settle down, and have four kids, strategically spaced two years apart. And what better place to meet all these God-fearing guys than in Bible college? Although there was nothing bad about these desires, I felt like a rebel for thinking outside the Susie-homemaker box. Was it wrong of me to aspire to be a youth pastor, or should I just want to marry one? Should my burning desire to be used by God be replaced by a burning desire to have a family? Could I do both? Did my anatomy somehow negate my calling?

During this season, I annoyed my professors. I interrupted lectures to drill them with questions about women in ministry, submission, marriage—you name it. Part of me felt I should sit down and be quiet. (Doesn't the Bible say this somewhere?) But there was a conviction in my gut that things weren't meant to be this way. It wasn't that I didn't want to be a wife and a mom. I just wasn't convinced that was the finish line. No one on campus would admit it, but the culture around me screamed differently.

Kings and Queens

The role of men and women can't be defined by a few verses Paul wrote for a specific culture and church community. If we desire to understand God's intent for humanity, we must go back to the beginning, before the fall.

Then God said, "Let us make mankind in our image, in our likeness, so that *they* may rule over the fish in the sea and the birds in the sky, over the livestock and all the wild animals, and over all the creatures that move along the ground."

Genesis 1:26, italics added

God's first agenda was for men and women to rule over creation *together*. The Hebrew word is *radah*, a royal term meaning to reign and have dominion. Imagine the final scene in the movie *The Chronicles of Narnia*. The four children enter the palace, dressed in regal garb escorted by the lion Aslan, who represents Jesus. They proceed toward four thrones as Aslan crowns Queen Lucy the Valiant, King Edward the Just, Queen Susan the Gentle, and King Peter the Magnificent. Each possessed unique attributes, but all were called to rule and reign *together*—and so are we.

So God created mankind in his own image, in the image of God he created them; male and female he created them.

Genesis 1:27

Both males and females reflect the image and likeness of God. One was not created less than, nor does one have more intrinsic value. God never designed one to rule over the other, but for us to work side by side. The word *helpmate* used to describe Eve was not referring to an administrative assistant or a glorified housekeeper. Rather, it was a military term for an allied king coming to the aid of a nation during a time of war. God's dream all along was for us to be co-laborers in Eden, ruling and reigning together. The mention of men lording over women or women trying to overthrow men's authority only came after the curse. And although sin has entered the picture and this power struggle may be a present reality, the Bible is a love

God never intended us to settle for the curse.

story of Jesus restoring what was lost in the garden. God never intended us to settle for the curse.

> God blessed them and said to them, "Be fruitful and increase in number; fill the earth and subdue it."
>
> Genesis 1:28

I fear our duty as women to multiply is often interpreted as our need to find a good man, get hitched, and have lots of babies. But if we narrow our calling to this role, we fail to honor Jesus' last words to his disciples and the many women who followed him:

> All authority in heaven and on earth has been given to me. There-fore go and make disciples of all nations, baptizing them in the name of the Father and of the Son and of the Holy Spirit, and teaching them to obey everything I have commanded you.
>
> Matthew 28:18–20

What if multiplication is more than how many matching outfits are posing in your family photo? What if it's a call to reproduce what God has done in our lives in the lives of others?

Jesus was notorious for breaking the religious rules of his day. One of his favorite cultural norms to reject was how women were treated by Jewish men. Men were not allowed to look at or address a woman in public. The women in turn were expected to remain silent and only speak with their husbands in the privacy of their homes. Yet Jesus walks through the ghetto (Samaria) and meets a woman at a well. He not only speaks to her but requests a drink. Then he delivers a word of knowledge in regard to her one too many husbands and reveals himself as the Messiah. The woman—transformed by this one encounter—runs back home, blabbing to everyone who will listen. Her entire town comes to faith in one day, all because she dared to open her mouth and share her story.

And what was Jesus' response?

Wake up and look around. The fields are already ripe for harvest.
The harvesters are paid good wages, and the fruit they harvest is
people brought to eternal life.

John 4:35–36 NLT, italics added

The fruit of our lives is more than how many mouths we feed.
The harvest is lives radically changed. And how will they hear
if we don't open our mouths and share our God stories? What
if there is a calling beyond the four walls of our home we have
been neglecting?

Maybe you've felt the void I'm talking about. You love your
husband. You adore your kids. But it feels like something is missing. Or maybe you're forty and single and you've spent twenty
years waiting for Mr. Right to come along so your life can begin.

Listen to me, you have a great destiny in God.

You didn't miss it.

There is more.

I may sound a bit extreme. But like the Samaritan woman, I
can't shut up. An encounter with Jesus will do that to you.

Running Mad for Jesus

I sat on the bus alone, wedged up against the ice-cold window. I
swirled my finger through the fogged-up glass and drew a smiley
face—but I was anything but happy. I was forced by my parents
to attend a Christian camp for a week. I felt like Tim Robbins in
the movie *Shawshank Redemption*, on my way to death row. My
eyes glazed over as I stared out the window at the dotted lines
whizzing by.

I sure hope there are some cute boys at this camp.

My days were filled with swimming, gross food games, and—in
my defense—way too much free time for a fifteen-year-old *not*

to get in trouble. Each night there was a worship service. I didn't know what to expect. My only context for church was a Catholic mass. There was no priest, no robes, no pews. Just a few rows of folding chairs, a keyboard, and a short, skinny preacher with the most impressive unibrow I had ever seen.

The pastor spoke of knowing God personally. He preached on the power of the Holy Spirit. I sat half listening with my arms crossed in the back row.

How could someone know God?

How can I talk to God when he doesn't talk back?

I tapped my foot as my eyes wandered around the gymnasium. The speaker asked if someone in the room was dyslexic. A girl stepped forward. A group of students placed their hands on her shoulder and began to pray. This scene was foreign to me. Prayer was something you promised to do but never followed through on. Or if you did, it happened late at night when you couldn't sleep while staring at your ceiling fan.

With a Bible opened in front of the dyslexic girl, the pastor and students cried out to God. After twenty minutes, my stomach grumbled and I snuck out of the gym doors to scope out the vending machine.

If this prayer thing is going to take forever, I need a snack.

I pressed B5, grabbed my Fritos, and reentered the gym to watch the show. Then something mind-blowing happened. The young girl burst into tears and started speed-reading the book of Genesis.

Everything around me transitioned into slow-mo. I fought back the tears. A part of me wanted to bawl my eyes out, while the other half of me wanted to sprint out of the gym.

It's real. It's all real. God's real.

Other campers around me wiped their tears with their sleeves. It was as if love had been boiled down into liquid form and was poured over my head, filling my body. I loved the girl who was healed, even though I didn't know her name. I loved the smelly, obnoxious kid sitting in the folding chair next to me. And I loved Jesus. I don't know how. I don't even know why. It was as if I had run into an old childhood friend—a friend I forgot existed.

When I returned home, I blabbed the story to every person who would listen. I ran up and down my dead-end street shouting. If I didn't do something, it felt like I was going to explode.

I may sound a bit extreme. But like the Samaritan woman, I can't shut up. An encounter with Jesus will do that to you.

Jesus' Groupies

In a society where women weren't allowed to learn, don't you find it strange Jesus had disciples who were women? In Jewish culture, women's duties consisted of preparing meals and caring for their families. Yet Jesus taught, affirmed, and encouraged women to follow him and sit at his feet—a position reserved only for students. And Jesus, like all good rabbis, expected his students to not only learn from him but to *do what he did*.

> Jesus traveled about from one town and village to another, proclaiming the good news of the kingdom of God. The Twelve were with him, and also some women who had been cured of evil spirits and diseases: Mary (called Magdalene) from whom seven demons had come out; Joanna the wife of Chuza, the manager of Herod's household; Susanna; and many others.
>
> Luke 8:1–3

Do you remember the story where Mary sat at Jesus' feet and her sister Martha was angry?[1] Martha wasn't mad at Mary for being lazy and refusing to help her bake barley bread. Martha was furious because Mary was neglecting her cultural role in the kitchen. Instead, she sat in the male quarters of the home, learning from Jesus. Mary boldly inserted herself into Jesus' innermost circle. And what does Jesus have to say about it?

Mary has chosen the good portion, which will not be taken away from her.

Luke 10:42 esv

Jesus honored Mary for choosing the better portion. He didn't say, "Mary, you've made a better *choice*." Rather, Jesus used a Greek word that meant inheritance. There is no better portion in life than following Jesus—doing what he did, teaching what he taught, and living how he lived. Motherhood is a divine responsibility, but may it never trump our calling to sit at Jesus' feet.

Far too many women believe they are a decoration for their husband's arm rather than a disciple at Jesus' feet. But God created us with a voice and a unique calling separate from our role as a wife and a mom. Our role as a mom is *part* of our calling, but our calling can never be defined by a single role. Even the term *pastor's wife* confuses me. My husband used to be a mailman. Imagine if I walked around referring to myself as the mailman's wife. How foolish would it be to think *his* job defined *me*? Only one Man defines me. And that Man created each of us with a calling and purpose before time began.[2]

Toilet Paper Queen

I plopped down at the kitchen table in my flannel pj's with a giant bowl of Frosted Flakes. I pulled my hair up into a messy bun and grabbed the *Free Trader*. Chewing on the end of my pen, I scanned the help-wanted ads while complaining.

This is not what I signed up for, Jesus.

After we moved home, I had no clue what our next steps looked like. I landed two dead-end jobs. By day, I was a glorified housekeeper, wiping pubic hair off toilets at a local hotel. At night, I worked for a newspaper company. Don't get too excited. I wasn't a reporter or writer. I was a stuffer. If you've ever grabbed a newspaper by the fold, a dozen flyers fall and land at your feet.

Believe it or not, somebody places those flyers into the centerfold, and that somebody was little ol' me. I knew I wasn't called to the newspaper-stuffing business, and I regretted ever leaving college.

Grasping for some sort of purpose, I contacted my youth pastor and asked to volunteer. I imagined he would schedule me to preach sermons and teach classes. Instead, he asked if I would be willing to clean the downtown youth center on a weekly basis. *More toilets. Thanks, Jesus.*

One fall afternoon, I stuffed my car with twenty-seven rolls of toilet paper and headed downtown. I parked across the road and crossed the street with a massive armful of TP. Several rolls slipped out of my arms and landed on the blacktop. As I chased down my runaway toilet paper, a voice called my name.

"Hey, Jess."

My head shot up and I found myself face-to-face with an old friend from high school.

"Hey, Jen. How are you?" I asked, feeling my face turn flush.

"I'm good. What are you up to these days?" she said as she handed me the roll of toilet paper with a smirk.

"Besides chasing toilet paper, not much," I said.

My friend shared that she had attended nursing school and was working toward becoming a physician's assistant. I'm fuzzy on the details. Her mouth was moving but I hit the mute button. I felt like such a loser. I assumed if I obeyed the Holy Spirit and moved home, something grand would be waiting for me. Instead, it was one humble job after another. If there was a crown prepared for me in heaven, I'm pretty sure it was made of toilet paper.

Not Another Sex Talk

Six months later, our youth pastor asked to meet with Greg and me. We walked into his study and sat at the edge of our seats. I squirmed like a kid in the principal's office as I stared at the books and pictures around the room. The last time we met in his office was our final session of premarital counseling—the birds and bees talk.

He plopped onto his worn-out computer chair, folded his hands, and leaned back.

"Do you know why I'm meeting with you?"

"Not really," Greg said.

"I'm planting a church in Vermont, and I'd like you two to take over the youth ministry."

My jaw dropped.

"We'll have to pray about it," Greg said, looking over at me.

I nodded.

Our pastor continued, "We would hire Jessica full time since she is pursuing her ministry degree, but we would want you to be involved too, Greg."

Greg's shoulders slumped—it was an ego check. He never pictured himself working for a church, but I'm not sure he wanted to be referred to as the youth pastor's husband either. (That would be weird.)

> Faith is a conscious decision to say yes despite all the no's around you.

We spent a few days praying and mulling over the pros and cons. We understood what a huge responsibility it was. Our feelings were all over the place. But faith isn't a feeling. Faith is a conscious decision to say yes despite all the no's around you. We were ill-equipped, unprepared, and unqualified—but we said yes anyway. Yes is the qualifier of the kingdom.

"I Gave You a Mouth—Use It"

I struggled with deep insecurity for years as a youth pastor. Then one August day, God showed me the power of my voice. I packed up my kids and headed to the beach. The sun peeked through the clouds as I climbed out of my minivan, and I rummaged through my purse for my sunglasses. I slipped off my flip-flops, shook the sand off my beach towel, and sat down at the water's edge.

"Emma, don't splash," I yelled as the lifeguard turned my way.

I was about to settle in with a good book until I realized my daughter had stolen a ball from an adorable brown-eyed boy. I pried the blue ball out of her hand and threw it to the cutie onshore.

"I'm sorry," I mouthed to his mother standing nearby.

There was something vaguely familiar about the boy. As I sat down on my beach towel, a memory flashed in my mind of a youth service years prior.

"Hey, Chelsea!" I greeted the student who approached me after the service wrapped up. All I wanted to do was go home, order Chinese takeout, and watch the newest episode of Lost.

"My friend is getting an abortion tomorrow morning."

My first response was to shoot up a quick prayer, ask God to intervene, and call it a night. But the Holy Spirit whispered to my heart:

I gave you a mouth—use it.

"Well, we've got twelve hours. Let's go find her," I said.

Surprised by my reaction, Chelsea grabbed her Bible and jumped in my car.

As we pulled into the driveway at Chelsea's friend's house, my headlights shone on an older woman cleaning out her car. The woman was the mom of Chelsea's friend. On an adrenaline rush, I busted open the car door while Chelsea slunk further into her seat.

I have no clue what I'm going to say, Jesus. I'm trusting you for the words.

"Hi. You don't know me. I'm a youth pastor. Your daughter is pregnant and is heading to an abortion clinic tomorrow. She confided in her friend that she's afraid of disappointing you."

Stunned, the woman stared at me as the words sunk in. Tears slipped from her eyes as she grabbed my hand.

"Thank you."

I climbed back in my car and sped away. A million questions ran through my mind.

Did I do the right thing? Is this any of my business?

As we drove away, I caught a glimpse of the mom and her daughter hugging in my rearview mirror. She never made it to the abortion clinic. A year later, I stumbled across a picture of her beautiful brown-eyed boy on Facebook. He was the same boy who smiled and waved at me from the water's edge as I threw him his blue ball.

PRAY THIS: *Dear Jesus, I'm sorry I've been hiding in the shadows. I foolishly believed humility required me to shrink back rather than step forward. I don't need the spotlight, but I long to be a good steward of all you have given me. Heal the insecurity in my heart. Teach me my voice matters as you hand me the microphone.*

DO THIS: Find an avenue or ministry you can contribute to. If you have a husband, sit down and have a conversation. Share your heart. Share your dreams. Don't hold back. Be brutally honest. Then pray and ask Jesus to give you one baby step toward finding your voice. Maybe you could start a blog to encourage Christian women. Maybe you could serve your church with your God-given talents. Maybe you could start a Bible study or moms' group in your home. Maybe you could find a teen or young adult who needs a mentor.

God has more for your life.

Your voice matters.

Take the mic, my friend.

TO THE MOM WHO CAN'T KEEP HER EYES OPEN:

I know it feels like someone took a pizza cutter and went to town, only leaving you with a tiny sliver. Between the 2:00 a.m. feedings, the meal prep, and the constant whining—you're hanging by a thread. You may not feel it, but you're blessed. God will give you more than you can handle. It's the only way he can move you from a place of self-sufficiency to God-reliance. Trust the process.

4

The Energy Drain

*Jesus, teach me
to lay down my life*

To this end I strenuously contend with all the *energy* Christ so
powerfully works in me.

—Colossians 1:29, italics added

I climbed onto the rose-colored exam table for my postnatal
checkup. The tick of the second hand rang in my ears as I chewed
my cuticles. My husband stood in the waiting room, swaying the
car seat back and forth in a futile attempt to mimic our baby
swing. I could hear my three-month-old son, Jeremiah, cry from
the exam room all the way down the hall. It made me anxious to
be away from him for even a few minutes.

Finally, the doctor entered, staring at a clipboard.

"Everything looks good. Your body healed well. And by the
way, you're pregnant."

"What? How does that happen?"

The doctor raised his eyebrows, "Do you really need me to explain how it happens?"

"I guess not," I said as my face lit up like my son's Playskool Glo Worm.

"Your due date is March 31," the doctor continued.

This was the same due date I received for my son a year prior. Irish twins. Except, I didn't want twins.

I can barely handle one, Jesus.

I proceed to take my walk of shame past the doctor and into the waiting room.

"How did it go?" my husband asked.

"We're having another baby," I said, trying to hold back the tears.

Greg looked down at our son fussing in his car seat and gazed back up at me.

> God doesn't seem to reference OUR plans when he makes HIS.

"How are we going to do this?" he said.

"I have no idea."

I cried on and off for two weeks. I felt guilty for not celebrating the new life God blessed us with. Countless women spend decades trying to conceive, while I was crying in my Cheerios because I was Fertile Myrtle. I desired a big family, but one child on top of the other was not how I planned it. However, God doesn't seem to reference *our* plans when he makes *his*.

The Selfishness Test: Parenting

Do you want to know how selfish you are? Have a baby. Don't get me wrong, the minute I held my son, it was love at first sight. My world faded into the background. My petty problems, my workout routine, and my five-year plan felt like useless information. I realized fulfillment is found when we give ourselves away. But at the same time, dry shampoo and I were best friends. There was a permanent indent on our rocking chair cushion the exact shape of my rear end due to the countless hours nursing him. I wore the same leggings and hoodie three days in a row, caked with spit-up and rice cereal.

Yet Jeremiah's first year was the best year of my life.

The most beautiful lesson of motherhood is this: the cost of dying to yourself yields the greatest return on your investment.

Jesus utilizes parenting to lead us into this truth: when we give up our lives—we find them. When we lay down our dreams—we discover them. When we serve our family—we unearth ourselves. But man, it's draining. Yet it is an end-of-the-day exhaustion that feels strangely satisfying. Why? Purpose exists outside of oneself. But here is the problem: as moms, we tend to pitch our tent at Camp Motherhood. We experience the fulfillment of motherhood and think:

This is what I was made for.

Motherhood is a pair of glasses gifted to us by our Creator enabling us to view the people around us through a different lens. Each person is a child of God—a child Jesus died for—and he calls us to die to ourselves to reach them. Parenting is like training wheels. God teaches us to find our bearings as we learn to live for someone else. But I don't see many grown-ups cruising downtown on kiddie bikes with training wheels.

> The cost of dying to yourself yields the greatest return on your investment.

Training wheels are for a season.

Motherhood is a season.

Eventually, Jesus desires to grab his wrench, loosen the bolts, and launch us into the world as he jogs beside us yelling, "You've got this!"

Punching Old Ladies

I'll never forget the first Sunday I conquered the feat of attending church after my daughter Mara was born. Sleep deprived, I dressed both the babies in coordinating outfits and buckled them up in their car seats so I could finish getting ready.

I've got this.

Little did I know, while I was applying concealer to hide my dark circles, my two cuties were concocting a plan to cause Mommy to lose her mind. I got a whiff of this plan as I passed the nursery.

Why do poop explosions always happen when you're heading out the door?

My husband walked out of our bedroom.

"Are you ready?"

"No," I said as I burst into tears. "I can't do this."

It wasn't a quick diaper change. Both babies had the poop-up-the-back-as-you-peel-off-the-onesie kind of diaper change. Both had to be bathed and redressed. I finally showed up to church thirty minutes late with my face still flushed. I regretted not applying a few extra swipes of deodorant. I set the car seats to the right and left of my feet and tried to enjoy the last five minutes of worship. I prayed all three of us wouldn't start crying.

During the offering, an elderly woman grabbed my arm.

"When you're old, you'll miss these days. God will never give you more than you can handle."

It took all my willpower to restrain myself from slapping her hand as she played with my daughter's feet. Maybe some well-intentioned woman told you the same thing at some point in your mothering career. And maybe you wanted to throw a right hook too.

Do you know this verse isn't even in the Bible? Can you imagine consoling the apostle Paul after he was beaten, stoned, shipwrecked three times, and imprisoned: "Don't worry Paul, God won't give you more than you can handle."

It's a flat-out lie.

But you probably shouldn't smack old ladies in church—even if they lie to you.

Conserving Energy

I thought I was tired caring for one baby. More experienced moms advised me to nap when he napped. Conserve your energy, they said. But when my daughter Mara was born nine months later, sleep was a luxury—like French manicures—I couldn't afford. Every night my son Jeremiah woke at one in the morning for a feeding. I tiptoed to his room. I cursed the creaking floorboard, cracked the door, and begged the angels to plug my little girl's ears so she would stay asleep. This never happened. Within five minutes, my daughter woke, screaming. And this vicious cycle continued until I didn't know what time it was, what day it was, or even what year it was.

Don't ever complain to the mom of a newborn that you're tired. She may lose it, grab the snot sucker from her diaper bag, and drive it through your temple like Jael did with the tent peg to that guy in the Old Testament.[1]

The old adage "God won't give you more than you can bear" is merely a twisted Bible verse. It's best fit for a throw pillow in the clearance aisle of TJ Maxx. The original verse reads like this:

> God is faithful; he will not let you be tempted beyond what you can bear. But when you are tempted, he will also provide a way out so that you can endure it.
>
> 1 Corinthians 10:13

The apostle Paul was instructing the church in Corinth to not waste their days complaining and indulging in sexual sin. He was reminding them that God would not allow the enemy to tempt us beyond what we can handle; he would provide an escape. This verse has nothing to do with motherhood or the overwhelm of life. Quite the contrary, God intentionally gives us more than we can handle.

Every summer, my son and his friends run around our neighborhood decked out in old Halloween costumes. Whether Spiderman, Batman, or the Hulk, each costume consists of cotton abs and perfectly-formed pecs. Eventually, the boys overheat, strip down to their scrawny sixty-pound bodies, and take a dip in the river behind our house.

May God use the fires of life and the weighty responsibility of parenting to strip us down to our scrawny selves. It's the only way Jesus can move us from a place of self-sufficiency to God-reliance.

Severed Pinkie Fingers

We pulled into the driveway with both babies crying in the back seat only to find twenty teenagers standing on our porch.

"What is going on?" I asked Greg.

"I have no clue," he said as he shifted the car into park.

"Is this some sort of joke?" I hollered to the teens as I swung open the door. (One time, the youth Saran wrapped everything in our house. They covered the couch, the TV, the salt and pepper shakers, our silverware, and even our cat in fifty-seven layers of plastic wrap. Okay, not the cat, but you can see why a prank was highly probable.)

"Surprise!" they yelled in unison.

I immediately went into panic mode. Had I forgotten my husband's birthday or an important date we should be celebrating because I was so sleep deprived?

"We want to clean your house, babysit, and treat you to dinner," one of the girls explained as she handed me a gift certificate to the Lobster House. "Reservations are at seven, so you better hurry."

I cried the whole twenty-minute car ride to the restaurant.

Something shifted in my heart that night.

I don't just need Jesus. I need people.

When we arrived, our table was set with a bouquet of roses and a card signed by all the teens. As an Enneagram Two, I aspire to be a mash-up of Mother Teresa and Michael Jackson. I strive to heal the world and make it a better place, but I can't seem to ask for help myself. Maybe you can relate. Maybe you're at your wit's end. But rather than picking up the phone and calling a friend, a babysitter, or your pastor, you Google an inspirational quote and post it on Instagram.

We were never meant to do this life alone. We are part of a whole.

But our bodies have many parts, and God has put each part just where he wants it. How strange a body would be if it had only one part! Yes, there are many parts, but only one body. The eye can never say to the hand, "I don't need you." The head can't say to the feet, "I don't need you." . . . All of you together are Christ's body, and each of you is a part of it.

1 Corinthians 12:18–21, 27 NLT

Christ is the head of the church. We are his body. Yet a lot of us function like a severed pinkie finger, flapping up and down on the pavement but getting nowhere. What if you're overtired and overworked because you're trying to do this life all by yourself? There is a remedy for this overwhelm, and it's not a Disneyland vacation or a trip to the spa—it's the body of Christ.

If you don't have a church to call your home, I want you to stop what you're doing and pull up Google. Type "local church in my area" and commit to finding one that preaches the Word of God faithfully and makes one-on-one discipleship a priority. Even if their worship is so-so, or the pews are hard, or you feel awkward—keep going until it feels like home. Surround yourself with other believers who can pray for you and encourage you. Find a spiritual mom or grandma to love your kiddos and lend a hand.

I read in a medical journal that a severed limb must be reattached within six to twelve hours of the injury. If a surgeon waits any longer, the tissue will deteriorate and die.[2] If something in you feels like it's dying, don't wait another week. Find a church to call your home.

Treating Felons to Pizza

My husband stretched out on the couch while I nestled between his feet and the armrest, sipping a Tim Horton's coffee. We relished a moment of silence—both babies asleep—until the buzz of his phone startled us.

Greg pulled the phone out of his pocket, stood to his feet, and paced the room. I tried to catch pieces of the one-sided conversation.

"What's wrong?"

"That was the police. Some kid from Teen Challenge stole money from the church. They caught him trying to buy a bus ticket a half a mile away," Greg said while walking toward the door.

"Where are you going?" I asked.

"To meet him. They want to know if we're going to press charges."

Each year, our church hosted a Teen Challenge team from Vermont. They spent a week hanging out in front of Walmart with business cards and plastic jugs for donations. On Sunday mornings, the young men shared stories of how God rescued them from addiction. The service always ended with a wad of tissues in my lap. We never had a problem—until now.

An hour later, my husband called.

"I won't be home for a while. I want to take him out to eat."

"Who?" I asked.

"The kid who stole from the church. He seems so sad—and hungry."

"Okay," I said. "Be safe."

I had a million questions, but I didn't ask a single one. At this point in our marriage, I trusted my husband's ability to follow God's lead. When the kingdom of God collides with your life—nothing makes sense. And I was learning to be okay with that.

Family First

I once watched a video of a pastor who had a rock collection. His goal was to fit all the rocks into one glass container.

Take One: He poured all the pebbles and sand into the jar and attempted to fit the larger rocks on top. Epic Fail.

Take Two: He removed all the smaller rocks and placed the large rocks in first. He poured the pebbles on top and finished with the sand. The sand filled the nooks and crannies of the jar, allowing for everything to fit into the glass container.

It was intended to be an illustration of how we need to keep our priorities straight. The three big rocks were labeled family, health, and friends. The smaller rocks symbolized other responsibilities such as work, sports, church, and hobbies. He taught that if we got our priorities straight, everything else would fall into place.

There's one problem with this analogy: it's not biblical.

Mister Rogers might tell you to put your family first, but Jesus isn't Mister Rogers. Jesus made some radical statements when it comes to our priorities. Things that if preached from a pulpit might cause the congregation to reinstitute stoning as corporal punishment. (Maybe that's why that pastor had a rock collection?)

> Then Jesus' mother and brothers arrived. Standing outside, they sent someone in to call him. A crowd was sitting around him, and they told him, "Your mother and brothers are outside looking for you." "Who are my mother and my brothers?" he asked. Then he looked at those seated in a circle around him and said, "Here are my mother and my brothers! Whoever does God's will is my brother and sister and mother."
>
> Mark 3:31–35

If I was Jesus' mom, I would be fuming. First he ignores her. (We all know how our kids have selective hearing.) Then she sends someone into the crowd to get his attention. Jesus acts as if his mother is not there while explaining to the crowd that they are more important than his own family.

Even worse, this was not an isolated incident. Jesus told his followers that unless they hated their parents, their family, and their own life, they were not fit to be his disciples.[3] Or how about the time Jesus went missing as a boy? Mary and Joseph traveled to Jerusalem to celebrate the Passover, and it took three days for them to notice Jesus was MIA. When they finally found him, he was hanging out in the temple with the rabbis.

When his parents saw him, they were astonished. His mother said to him, "Son, why have you treated us like this? Your father and I have been anxiously searching for you." "Why were you searching for me?" he asked. "Didn't you know I had to be in my Father's house?"

Luke 2:48–49

Once again, Jesus seems more concerned with serving his heavenly Father. So what does this mean for us as moms? Should we neglect our children and throw ourselves into ministry? Would Jesus glorify the workaholic father who never spends time with his family? Of course not. But it does mean that there is no such thing as family first in the kingdom of God.

Open Door Policy

Greg returned home later that night.

"What happened?" I asked.

Before he could respond, our front door creaked open and a young man with a buzz cut stood in the entryway. His pants sagged so far down, his plaid boxers were hanging out.

"This is Adam." My husband flashed a sheepish grin.

"Hi, Ad—"

"I'm sorry I stole the money," Adam said.

And without thinking I blurted, "It's okay."

For two hours, Adam sat at our dining room table, flipping through his sketchpad. He would show us a picture while simultaneously sharing a horrifying memory from his childhood. When his eyes watered, he flipped the drawing pad to a new page and changed the subject.

He wasn't a criminal. He was a broken little boy trapped in a grown man's body.

Then *it* happened. The still small voice of the Holy Spirit interrupted Adam's rant:

"Ask him to live with you," I felt Jesus speak to my heart.

72

You want me to ask a convicted felon who I just met, who is running from the law, who stole from our church, to live in our home with our two toddlers? Are you crazy, Jesus?

But Jesus *is* crazy—crazy in love with Adam.

A wellspring of love bubbled out of my heart. The same love I experienced at camp when I witnessed the girl healed of dyslexia. The same love I felt when I typed the instant message to Greg. This same love possessed me. It wasn't my love to claim. It was God's love, and I had a responsibility to do something with it. Love is just a feeling unless we act on it.

Freely you have received. Now freely give.[4]

When we finally crawled into bed at two in the morning, my husband rolled over and confessed, "I feel like we should ask him to live with us."

"That's what I was afraid you'd say. Let's talk in the morning."

I'm sure he was expecting an argument, a flat-out fight, or at least a reaction from me. But when two people are running hard after God, they tend to bump into each other.

Seek First His Kingdom

When we're exhausted physically, mentally, and emotionally, how do we muster up the energy to serve God? When our kids ask five hundred questions an hour, how do we find grace to serve the youth ministry on Wednesday nights? When you haven't slept in three days, how do you notice the poor woman in the checkout line who doesn't have enough money for cat food? How can we serve Jesus with our best when as a mom it feels as if we have nothing left?

Self-care gurus instruct us to put our own oxygen mask on first, and psychologists remind us that we can't pour from an empty cup. Hold tight to your time and spend it in moderation. Practice boundaries and time management.

Yet Jesus didn't teach us to conserve our energy but to waste it on him:

Seek first the kingdom of God and his righteousness, and all these things will be added to you.

Matthew 6:33 ESV

Jesus instructs us to spend our energy on serving him. Here lies the problem with modern-day Christianity: we want to sport our WWJD bracelets, but we don't want to do the outrageous things he did. I'm afraid we've settled for civilized Christianity. Christianity without the cross is just a glorified country club. We want to act like the rest of the world while maintaining high moral standards. I'm pretty sure the Pharisees felt the same way. Yet Jesus calls us to live radically different:

For whoever wants to save their life will lose it, but whoever loses their life for me will find it.

Matthew 16:25

It's not a matter of eliminating energy zappers but filling our time with kingdom work. The solution isn't moderation but adoration. Our deep love for God and the church was meant to crowd out the things of this world. And when it does? Jesus promises to take care of the rest.

House Guest Turned Son

Adam lived with us for a year. As parents, we think we love our kids because they have our DNA, our eyes, or our grandma's dimples. But roots of love grow when we make the conscious choice to pour our lives out for others.

What we water grows.

Adam stole our money *and* our hearts. He progressed from a felon, to a friend, to a son. Most mornings, I found him at our kitchen sink. He yearned to say thank you but didn't have the words—so he did the dishes instead. Adam gave his life to Jesus.

He joined a Christian support group called Celebrate Recovery and volunteered with our youth group. We hired him at our coffee shop and taught him the value of hard work, faith, and family.

On our first Christmas together, I gave him a frame with this verse:

God sets the lonely in families, he leads out the prisoners with singing.

Psalm 68:6

That frame sat on his nightstand. But the notion of family was a double-edged sword. He desired to belong, but our love was a constant reminder of what he missed out on as a kid. Part of him wanted to run. Part of him longed to stay. At one point, Adam got in trouble with the law and things went downhill. We never got to say goodbye. There was no happy ending. I wondered if we heard Jesus right. But God has a way of showing us in hindsight what we can't see in the middle of the mess.

A year after Adam left, we were on a road trip with our five-year-old son. He fell asleep in the car and startled awake when we stopped at a red light.

"Mom, I had the weirdest dream," Jer said.

"What?"

"I dreamt the world ended and our whole family was in heaven—well, except Dad," he explained.

"Where was Dad?" I laughed and punched Greg in the shoulder. "Do you have some secret sin you're hiding, honey?"

Greg rolled his eyes.

"Dad was on earth with Jesus helping him build a new earth," Jer said.

The air was sucked out of the car as Greg and I sat speechless.

"Did you learn about the new earth in kids' church?"

"No, what's that?" Jer said. "But the best part, Adam was with us in heaven."

That road trip and dream taught me a vital lesson: With God, nothing is ever wasted.

I received a text yesterday that Adam passed away. He was thirty years old. We still aren't sure if it was an overdose or suicide. The last text he sent me reminds me that our love for others makes a difference, even when we don't see it:

> I miss you guys. Sometimes when I feel like this I want to talk to my mom. I know it's not possible so I write you messages and don't send them. I'm sending this one though. I love you and Greg.

I wondered why I couldn't finish this chapter, but now I know God wanted to have the final word. I know one day we will meet again. And when we do, Adam will be at the door of the Hurlbut house in heaven, waiting to welcome his family home.

Waste your energy on the kingdom—because with God nothing is ever wasted.

PRAY THIS: *Dear Jesus, I'm spent. Forgive me for trying to be a mom, a wife, and a Christian in my own strength. Bring me to the end of myself until I fall to my knees and realize my desperate need for you. I can't do this life on my own. Teach me how to put you first in my life, even before my kids and spouse. Help me invest my energy not only into my family, but into your kingdom.*

DO THIS: If you don't attend church, find a local body of believers and commit to attend this coming Sunday. Google "Local churches in my area."

Once you find one, don't be a spectator. Invite someone over for coffee. Volunteer to serve as a greeter or in kids' church. Start a mom's group.

Seek God.

Build the church.

And find your place in the body of Christ.

TO THE MOM WITH THE NEGATIVE BANK ACCOUNT:

Jesus knows the ache in your heart when your kids go without. He notices the long hours you put in and every sacrifice you make. It may feel like you're carrying the weight of the world on your shoulders, but the burden is God's to carry. His yoke is only easy when you shift the weight toward him and train your heart to trust.

5

The Pinch of Finances

*Jesus, cut the ties money
has on my heart*

God never leads anyone anywhere for money.

—Jack Hyles

God sees every calculated decision you make regarding money. He notices when you fill your cart with groceries only to place items back on the shelf as you tally the bill in your head. He knows when you're stressed about paying the mortgage, the gas bill, and the electric bill and how it's impossible to cover them all. He hears your desperate petitions as you drive to work, praying your car runs off fumes until your next paycheck. If we were at a coffeeshop together, I would grab your hand, look you in the eyes, and remind you that even though prices are rising and gas is through the roof—God is *still* on the throne.

God promises to provide our daily bread, but most days, this doesn't cut it. We often think, *Okay Jesus, you've got today covered. I'll just worry about the future. And my kids' future. And their college debt. And my retirement fund. And the loan we took out for that new boat. And the rising cost of baby formula. And the rate of inflation.*

> Even though prices are rising and gas is through the roof—God is still on the throne.

And the list goes on and on. It's as if God's provision is a truth which exists in our heads but never drops the eighteen inches to our hearts.

We don't like to talk about money. It feels too personal, too vulnerable, too messy. So we mull over these things in our minds, wondering if anyone else feels the same way. Yet God sees every one of our financial struggles, and guess what? He's not limited by them. Unfortunately, it took me years of striving before I learned this lesson.

A Christmas without Presents

"What's wrong?" my husband asked as I slunk further into the passenger seat.

I turned and stared out the window, trying to hide my tears.

"Do you want something from Taco Bell?" he asked as we pulled up to the drive-thru, pretending not to notice my red cheeks and watery eyes.

"No."

Honestly, I *was* hungry but had reverted to penny-pinching mode. It was a week before Christmas. We had wandered around the mall searching for the perfect gifts, yet we left empty handed.

The problem?

Our total budget for both children was fifty dollars. Money was tight. The ache in the pit of my stomach was too familiar. It was the same knot I experienced as a girl when I went without and found myself too afraid to ask for help. Now not only was I struggling, my kids were too.

This was a defining moment in the Taco Bell parking lot. (I know, not the greatest location to have a defining moment.) That day an ungodly belief took root in my heart, and it sounded like this: *There's never enough.*

It's not our lack of finances that stops God from using us. Rather, it's our agreement with these ungodly beliefs that causes us to take matters into our own hands.

We work harder and longer.

We settle for jobs we hate.

We make decisions about money we're ashamed of.

And we omit anything God calls us to do that doesn't add to the bottom line.

When we operate in the spirit of never enough, we inevitably shelve our callings. The enemy whispers, "You can serve God after you earn more money, land the promotion, or your husband finds a job with better health benefits. Then you'll be free to run after all God has for you." But if we wait too long, we'll find ourselves taking advantage of our senior citizen's discount, sipping coffee, and staring out a diner window full of regrets.

> We don't have a finance problem, but a heart problem.

The truth is, we don't have a finance problem, but a heart problem.

The Man Dressed in Black

Money isn't evil.

It's the love of it that trips us up.

I can't count the number of times my husband has sat with a couple to present to them a ministry position, only to have them decline. Their hearts burn for the things of God. But when he lays out the time commitment, the cost, and the subpar salary—they're unable to say yes to the very thing they know God has called them to.

Why? Finances.

No one can serve two masters. Either you will hate the one and love the other, or you will be devoted to the one and despise the other. You cannot serve both God and money.

Matthew 6:24

As humans, we think we are the exception and others are the rule.

Most people don't consider themselves rich. But over half the world's population lives on less than two dollars and fifty cents a day.[1] Whether you feel like it or not, you *are* rich. But we think the wealthy are living in Silicon Valley with their Teslas, at-home espresso machines, and live-in nannies. *Those people* love money more than they love God. Not us.

Do you know you can love money even when you don't have any?

Sometimes, this is when we find ourselves obsessing over it the most. But Jesus reminds us we can't serve God and money. When we envision the word *serve*, we picture the person at Olive Garden who brings us our food. But the Greek word for *serve* is best defined as "to be a slave to."

Ouch.

> Do you know you can love money even when you don't have any?

Imagine standing before two masters: One adorned in a white robe, arms stretched, beaming with love. The other clothed in black, hunched over, with beady eyes glaring out from under his hood. Which one would you choose to serve? A good Father who promises to provide all you need? Or an evil master who continually enslaves you in the vicious cycle of striving for more?

We will always be slaves to money if the overhead speakers of our lives are blaring the song "Never Enough."

Believing You're a Bother

"Hurry up, we're going to be late," my sister hollered as she slammed the door.

I slung my book bag over my shoulder, cracked open the kitchen cupboard, and peered into the change jar. Rummaging through a pile of pennies, I unearthed three dimes and a nickel.

Ugh, not enough.

School lunches cost one dollar, and most days the change jar didn't cover the expense.

I ran out the door and climbed into the car with my sister and dad.

"What's wrong with you?" my sister asked.

"Nothing."

I sat in silence for the rest of the car ride. Rather than asking my dad for a dollar, I chose to go without. I grew up in a large family. Although we were not rich by any means, my parents would not be okay with one of us going hungry.

The problem was a breakdown in communication.

I decided early on never to ask for anything. Not because my parents didn't love me, but because I believed I was a bother. Most days, I sat at the cafeteria table with my stomach growling while my friends stuffed their faces. Never once did I ask for help; instead, I got really good at pretending. (There was one boy in high school who felt bad for me. He asked his mom for an extra dollar to buy me lunch. That boy's name was Greg Hurlbut.)

The lies we believe as kids can morph into ungodly beliefs. We strap them on like backpacks and carry them around for the rest of our lives. Believing I was a bother was the number one soundtrack on repeat in my head.

I bet you can relate. Maybe you desire to stay home with your kids, but it feels impossible financially. You don't dare sit down and have a conversation with your husband. Maybe you yearn to work outside the home. But it feels like a selfish request when the cost of childcare negates any money you may earn. So we suffer in silence.

Why is money so hard to talk about, even with those we love?

Maybe it's because money and our hearts are so tightly intertwined. Jesus said:

> For where your treasure is, there your heart will be also.
>
> Matthew 6:21

Conversations about money are comparable to placing our hearts on a table and handing someone a sledgehammer. Plus, in America, we're taught to be independent. We build our fences, we demand our privacy, and we hide our problems. Many of us could never fathom approaching our churches, our family, or God when we're in a bind. Yet the book of James reminds us:

> You do not have because you do not ask.
>
> James 4:2

Maybe there is something to this whole asking thing.

Just-Because Gifts

I have a friend who is the queen of just-because gifts. When we go to coffee—she gives me a gift. If I accompany her to a doctor's appointment—she hands me a thank-you card. If I have a rough day—an encouraging card will be in my mailbox. Just-because gifts remind us we are seen and loved.

God is the king of just-because gifts.

My first just-because gift arrived in December 1995. I was a bratty junior higher with boys on the brain. I did *not* deserve this gift.

But we never deserve just-because gifts.

I was counting down the days until my school trip to Boston. The only problem? A deposit of two hundred dollars was due. Two hundred dollars my parents didn't have.

I pitched a fit and threatened to run away. I only made it to the end of the driveway. As I plunked myself on the curb with my Jan-Sport book bag in tow, my older sister walked out and sat beside me. As a means to cheer me up, she offered to treat me to bingo.

Side note: To be master at bingo, you need three things:

1. More cards than one can humanly scan.
2. A lucky charm (a troll with rainbow hair is recommended).
3. To chant the number you're waiting on until you win.

I followed this strategy to a tee, yet I never yelled bingo. By the last game of the night, I was desperate. So I did something you probably shouldn't do. I asked God to let me win. I wasn't sure if Jesus liked gambling, but I was pretty sure he liked me.

The final game required you to fill the entire bingo card. I was waiting on one number, N 43. As I chanted the number softly, an old man's muffled voice boomed through the speaker, "N 43."

I shot out of my seat and ran to the front. I had won the last game of the night.

And the prize?

$200.

The exact amount I needed for my school trip.

You might call this blind luck. Or maybe you can look past the foolishness of a twelve-year-old girl and see a God who cares about every little need we have.

Jesus reminds us in Matthew 7:7–8, 11:

Ask and it will be given to you; seek and you will find; knock and the door will be opened to you. For everyone who asks receives; the one who seeks finds; and to the one who knocks, the door will be opened. . . . If you, then, though you are evil, know how to give good gifts to your children, how much more will your Father in heaven give good gifts to those who ask him!

God has been a dad for a long time. He's pretty good at it. He cares about the smallest worry we obsess over and the biggest heartache we face. He anticipates our needs before we ask. But he waits on us to initiate the process.

How many just-because gifts are stored in heaven unopened with your name on the tag? How many times is God sitting on the edge of his throne, waiting to answer your prayers, but you never open your mouth?

You don't have to earn it.

He wants to bless you—just because.

Prisoner of Practicality

The summer before my senior year of high school, I surrendered my future plans to God. On the cold gym floor of a Christian camp with tears streaming down my face, I whispered, "Whatever you want, Jesus."

My heartfelt response felt straightforward and simple.

But everything feels simple when your mom is your Uber driver and the only money you manage is your allowance.

Yet the older we grow, the more complicated life becomes.

First comes love.

Then comes marriage.

Then comes Jessica pushing a baby carriage two double strollers. In six years, our family was blessed with five kids. Things got *really* complicated. Most days, I felt like a drunk driver swerving over the white line as I tried to navigate motherhood, ministry, and money.

We know God has more for us, but we can't fathom how to make room in the cracks of life. Whether you're a homeschool mom planning science projects during the day while running a side hustle at night, or you work a nine-to-five job to make ends meet while wishing to be home with your kids, most of us are familiar with the stress of finances.

A friend of mine described this tension perfectly. When asked why it felt impossible for him to quit his job—a job he despised—and pursue God's will for his life, he said something I'll never forget.

"I'm a prisoner of practicality."

Practicality is the actual doing of something rather than an idea or theory. Our spirits yearn to break free and run after God. But our mortgages, health insurance, and car loans shackle us to a man-made prison of practicality.

When my husband and I were newlyweds, I earned five hundred dollars a week. We survived on massive amounts of ramen noodles and crumbs of faith. I desired to serve our youth ministry, but paying our bills felt more urgent than investing in the next generation. I wanted to volunteer at VBS, grab a coffee with a young adult, or make a meal for a sick friend, but I found myself continually saying no. One night, I was complaining to God, asking him to make a way for me to serve more. Immediately my thoughts were interrupted by a question. Jesus is notorious for answering questions with questions.

"If a stranger offered you five hundred dollars a week to disobey me—would you?"

"Absolutely not," I said.

"Then don't you dare let the spirit of never enough talk you out of following me."

Walking Away Sad

I don't believe in luck, fate, or that some people are born with a silver spoon in their mouth. I believe each day presents us with divine opportunities to say yes. Jesus is playing tug of war with every human soul and posing one question: "Will you follow me?"

There is a story in the Bible of a rich dude who stops Jesus on his way to Jerusalem to ask what it takes to earn a spot in heaven. Jesus—knowing money was his weak spot—asks him to sell all he owns and follow him.

The man refused. And this is the line that gets me: "The man's face fell. He went away sad, because he was very rich" (Mark 10:22 NIrv).

And here is the kicker, Jesus kept walking.

Jesus won't beg you to follow him.

He won't twist your arm or guilt trip you into it.

He just keeps walking.

I don't believe Jesus had twelve disciples because they were the chosen few. I think Jesus had twelve disciples because he asked hundreds to follow him and only twelve said yes. We don't need to be talented to follow Jesus, we just need to be available.

A lack of money isn't holding us back from pursuing all God has for us. It's not the *lack* of money, but the *love* of money that puts a cap on our ability to be used by God. Paul warns his protégé Timothy:

> The love of money is a root of all kinds of evil. Some people, eager for money, have wandered from the faith and pierced themselves with many griefs.
>
> 1 Timothy 6:10

The root of a plant is unseen. It's like the operating system of a computer. We don't see it, but it's working behind the scenes, controlling the response of each function we perform on our MacBook. The same is true when we allow money to be first in our lives. It runs in the background, subconsciously determining our decisions and direction.

I'm not here to beat you up about your finances. We are experts at doing this ourselves. I'm here to dig up the root and ensure we are serving God and not the black-hooded demon of Never Enough.

I Can Have Money, But Money Can't Have Me

The best way to break our obsession with money is to give.

Newly married, we had a measly income, so the idea of giving was ridiculous to me. My husband, on the other hand, grew up in a Christian home that practiced tithing. The word *tithe* is first seen when Abraham offers a tenth of his spoil to the priest Melchizedek.[2] But this principle repeats again and again throughout the Bible. In the story of Cain and Abel, Cain presented *some* of his crops, while Abel offered the *best* of the lambs from his flock.

Cain gave his leftovers.

Abel gave his best.[3]

And don't we do this with God?

The word tithe means a tenth. Tithing is when we give 10 percent of our income to God through the means of a local church. Well-meaning Christians argue tithing isn't found in the New Testament. They counter that because Christ arrived on the scene, we no longer need to live under the law. And although this is true to an extent, Jesus seems to up the ante:

> If you refuse to take up your cross and follow me, you are not worthy of being mine. If you cling to your life, you will lose it; but if you give up your life for me, you will find it.
>
> Matthew 10:38–39 NLT

Jesus doesn't request 10 percent, but 100 percent. Yet most of the time, we give Jesus our leftovers. We toss a few dollars in the offering plate and call it a day. We never learn how to trust God as our Provider.

God doesn't *need* our money.

But he asks us to give.

Why?

When my kids were small, they would tear open their birthday gifts and try to yank the toy out of the box. After a few minutes of frustration, they would ask for help. I would whip out the scissors and cut the twist ties in the back that secured the toy to the cardboard. Giving cuts loose the hold money has on our hearts. We may tug and attempt to offer our lives to God, but giving—especially when it hurts—is the only way to free our hearts from the love of money. That's why God asks us to give. He doesn't want our money. He wants our hearts.

> **Giving cuts loose the hold money has on our hearts.**

There is a beautiful story in the Bible of an old widow who hobbled up to the offering jar and dropped in two mites. This would be equivalent to one-quarter of a penny. The two coins made a tiny clink as they hit the bottom. The noise was small on earth, but the sound reverberated in the throne room of heaven. Jesus stopped everything to draw attention to this woman.

> Truly I tell you, this poor widow has put more into the treasury than all the others. They all gave out of their wealth; but she, out of her poverty, put in everything—all she had to live on.
>
> Mark 12:43–44

So the next time someone argues that Jesus doesn't want us to give 10 percent, casually say, "You're right. He requires 100 percent."

Don't Spend Money You Don't Have

One of the best decisions my husband and I made about money was to attend a class by Dave Ramsey called Financial Peace University. It's a ten-week course that teaches biblical principles on how to handle money. One of Dave's famous lines is, "Debt is dumb." We know debt is stupid, but oftentimes the end justifies the means. My car is unreliable—insert car loan. A college education will get me places—come on in Sallie Mae. A home is an investment—hello, mortgage. When my husband and I totaled our debt, we owed more in monthly payments than we had cash coming in. For newlyweds, this was a recipe for disaster.

> The borrower is slave to the lender.
>
> Proverbs 22:7

Many of us are drowning in debt with no end in sight. We desire to follow Jesus, but when we take a step forward, we're jerked back by the financial shackles fastened to our ankles.

Prisoners of practicality.
Yet Jesus wants to teach us to trust him—not Mastercard.

Whatever I Place in God's Hand Multiplies

The scrawny boy plopped on the hillside with his Spiderman lunchbox nestled under his arm. He was daydreaming of how good his bologna sandwich would taste. (Okay, I know it wasn't a bologna sandwich, but if my son Isaac was telling this story, he would definitely be eating a bologna sandwich.) He kept his hands busy by plucking blades of grass and collecting them in his lap while listening to the rabbi. As usual, the teacher was long-winded.

"I'm hungry," the little boy whispered as he tugged on his mother's arm.

"Shhh. Not yet, buddy."

"Let's break for lunch," the rabbi said as if the boy's whisper had traveled on the wind and into the teacher's ear.

The boy flipped the lid of his lunchbox as one of the disciples stepped toward him.

"What's for lunch?" Peter asked.

"Just a bologna sandwich."

"Could we borrow it for Jesus?"

He looked up at his mom, wincing as he waited for her reply. "Of course, you can. Whatever the rabbi needs."

The boy's shoulders slumped. His eyes strained to follow his Spiderman lunchbox as it traveled toward Jesus. The teacher held the sandwich up toward the sky as his lips mumbled words the boy couldn't make out.

The nerve. He's thanking God for my sandwich.

The boy expected the rabbi to take a bite, but Jesus handed the sandwich back to his disciples. They proceeded to tear his lunch into pieces and distribute them to the crowd.

"What are they doing?" the boy asked his mom. "My sandwich can't feed two people, let alone five thousand."

Eventually, a piece of his sandwich landed in his lap, and then another, until he ate so much he felt as if his stomach would burst. Looking up at his mother, gleaming with pride, he said, "Jesus used *my* sandwich, Mom. *My* sandwich."[4]

"I know, honey. It's like your Father always says, 'What you keep—you lose. But what you give—God multiplies.'"

PRAY THIS: *Dear Jesus, I'm sorry for not trusting you with my finances. It's not my money, it's yours. Forgive me for operating in the spirit of never enough. Help me to believe I'm not a bother, but a blessing. Like the widow in the Bible, I want to spend everything I have on you. Loosen the grip the love of money has on my heart. I don't want to be a prisoner of practicality. I open my hands and give out of my lack, trusting you as my sole Provider.*

DO THIS: Start tithing. If you are married, have a conversation with your spouse. Tithing to your local church needs to be a joint decision. I know the idea of giving is terrifying in today's economy. But God can't display his provision and power if we hold on to everything and try to manage it ourselves. What you give—God multiplies.

TO THE MOM WHO FEELS ABANDONED:

I know you think God deserted you in your darkest hour. You cried out to him on that cross and nothing changed. Your loved one still died. The cancer still remained. Your child still struggled. Your marriage still ended. But don't let your feelings deceive you. God turned his back on his own Son so he would never have to turn his back on you.

6

The Pressure of Pain

Jesus, help me die to the why

> God whispers to us in our pleasures, speaks in our consciences,
> but shouts in our pains. It is his megaphone to rouse a deaf world.
>
> —C. S. Lewis, *The Problem of Pain*

"Stop it, Jess. If you bring up the A-word one more time, I'm going to lose it."

My husband rolled over with a grunt while yanking the comforter tight around his body. No goodnights exchanged. No I love you. Only the dead silence I had grown accustomed to. I lay staring up at the ceiling. This was *not* a new argument. We had played the silent treatment on and off for over a month. My daughter Mara was three years old and exhibited all the red flags of autism. Although we had no official diagnosis, I found myself determined to fix her. I ordered dozens of books from Amazon and watched every autism documentary on Netflix.

My husband, on the other hand? He inhabited a totally different world: The Land of Denial. He didn't want to talk about it, read about it, think about it, and God forbid I ever uttered the A-word.

If I was determined to *fix* it, he was determined to *forget* it.

Unable to sleep, I snuck out of bed. Stumbling into the kitchen, I withdrew to the one place I knew I could find answers: the Google search bar. A YouTube video popped up of a child hopping in front of a TV. I clicked play and immediately my suspicions were confirmed. The boy jumped and flapped with excitement as he listened to the opening song of his favorite show. The caption read "My Autistic Son Aiden." The clip lasted nine seconds, but I watched it over and over again. You could have swapped out his head with my daughter's. Their mannerisms and the bizarre noises they uttered were identical. I no longer needed an official diagnosis, genetic testing, or a trip to the developmental center.

I knew my daughter was autistic.

I closed my laptop and wandered back to my bedroom while this mantra played on repeat in my head:

If this is what I get for following you, Jesus, I'm out.

Something in me died that night.

I think it was hope. Maybe it was faith. I'm still not sure. But the void left behind was flooded with anger. Anger toward God. Anger toward my husband. Anger toward my kids. Anger toward the UPS guy who failed to deliver the kids' Halloween costumes on time. Anger toward the old lady in the Cadillac in front of me who took a decade to turn right and never used her blinker.

This uncontrollable rage was new to me. Good girls don't yell at God. Yet the pain of life snapped the strap which had bound my truckload of emotions for far too long. I was undone.

As I drifted off to sleep that night, with a wad of tissues surrounding my head like a halo, God turned the page of my story and forced me into a new chapter—a chapter with the bold title The Great Undoing.

The Invisible Pressure

Raising a child with severe autism is comparable to walking with a limp. Trips to the grocery store with my daughter ensure I will get *the look* when hobbling toward the door. It's guaranteed a stranger will dash to my rescue and open it. Their eyes fill with compassion. Few words are exchanged, but I know their internal dialogue.

Bless her heart.

There is nothing I despise more than the look.

We all have limitations. Some are pronounced, while others are whispered behind closed doors. Yet every limit is birthed from a point of pain.

When we get to heaven, instead of shows like *American Idol*, there will be contests for those who endured the most pain. If I have a say, the golden buzzer goes to the apostle Paul. He was whipped, beaten, stoned, robbed, imprisoned, and shipwrecked—not once, not twice, but three times. If anyone was qualified to put pen to paper regarding this unique experience, Paul was the man.

> We are hard pressed on every side, but not crushed; perplexed, but not in despair; persecuted, but not abandoned; struck down, but not destroyed.
>
> 2 Corinthians 4:8–9

But I *feel* crushed, Paul.

Maybe you do too. Maybe you replay the agony of saying good-bye to a loved one in an impersonal hospital room filled with tubes and wires. Maybe the marriage destined to last forever collapsed. You're left bumbling through your words as you attempt to explain the mess to your teary-eyed children. Maybe your teen has you at your wits' end and is nowhere near the young adult you dreamt they would be when you rocked them in your arms. Maybe it's the little things adding pressure to your soul—a promotion you toiled for only to be overlooked. Maybe it's the exhaustion you feel day in and day out as you care for the tiny humans under your roof.

Someone smart once said pain travels in waves while grieving the death of a loved one.

But in my life, pain never stops advancing. I pop my head above the water to catch a breath, and another wave smacks me in the face. Seasons change, but the rhythmic ebb and flow of pain is constant. Sometimes the waves are terrifying. Other times, the ripples gently clap against the boat of our lives.

> Pain either pushes you forward or pulls you back. The one thing pain does not do is leave you where you once were.

If you remember from eighth-grade science class, a force by definition is a push or a pull. Pain is a force. Pain moves you. Pain either pushes you forward or pulls you back. The one thing pain does not do is leave you where you once were.

To top it off, pain creates an invisible pressure. Each heartache stacks upon the next. You can stuff your sorrows for years, but they stubbornly refuse to vanish or resolve on their own—rather they build. Eventually, you find yourself like me, screaming curse words at the air while simultaneously handing God your letter of resignation.

I'm done with you, God.

His response?

He smirks and replies, "Good, now we can begin."

The Great Undoing

People always commented on my cool and collected nature. It took a lot to rattle me. So when I snapped, it scared me. I questioned my sanity. I didn't want to shower, wear anything but yoga pants, or associate with humans. I repeated for weeks to my husband that he should check me into a mental hospital. He laughed, which made me angry, because a part of me was serious.

Then came the doubts: *Am I even a Christian? How can God use someone this messed up? Have I wasted my life living for something that isn't real?*

Followed by guilt: *I am a pastor; I shouldn't be thinking these things. I should be stronger than this. Why is my faith so weak?*

When I surveyed my doubts, guilt, and lack of sanity—I had nothing to offer. If God had a baseball team, I would be the loser on the bench who was the last one to be picked.

But guess what? God loves picking the losers.

And as far as having nothing to offer? He likes that too.

I desired to crawl under my down comforter with an entire sleeve of Oreos and hide from the world. But unfortunately, when you're a mom, you can't run *or* hide. The everyday demands continued onward, even though I desperately needed a pause button. But the Great Undoing isn't the end of your *life*, rather the end of *yourself.* And when God escorts you to the end of yourself, he has a way of getting your attention.

Making Angels Jealous

The next morning, my husband slung his computer bag over his shoulder and headed off to church.

"Bye," I said, sprawled out on the floor playing with Mara.

He glanced my way and slammed the door. I returned my attention to my daughter. She crouched in front of the couch and lined up her toy cars end to end. My stomach churned—another sign of autism. I rummaged through the basket on the mantel, found the TV remote, and fought back the only way I knew how: worship. Blasting my favorite song, I raised my hands and closed my eyes.

You're the only One who can get me through this, Jesus.

I worshiped uninterrupted until my leg bumped into a warm body. My daughter had plunked down at my feet and peered upward with her arms extended. I scooped Mara up as she wrapped her tiny hands around my neck. I found myself caught in a divine moment. Rather than slithering from my grasp, she laid her head on my shoulder, and a strange peace cascaded over both of us. We rocked back and forth for fifteen minutes as the music swelled in the background.

The Great Undoing isn't the end of your LIFE, rather the end of YOURSELF.

Do you know there is a gift we can give God the angels are jealous of?

It's the gift of worshiping *despite* our pain. In heaven, we will understand all God's ways. But on earth, it's as if we are sitting in a dark room gazing in a mirror. What moves the heart of God more than the saints casting their crowns before the throne is a woman on earth who makes the conscious choice to worship *despite* her pain. This act captures all of heaven's attention.

Dwelling on the Why

Do you remember the game Twenty Questions? I like to play this game with God.

Why would you allow this? What did I do to cause Mara to be autistic? Was it my failure to eat truckloads of organic kale while pregnant? Or was it the day I changed the cat litter? Maybe it was the time I drank two cups of coffee in one day? Should I have refused all those vaccines?

His response? Silence.

God's not rattled by our interrogations. He desires us to be honest about our disappointments. I found myself yelling at God more times than I can count. He was the One who could fix this situation.

Why, God? Do you hear me? Do you even care?

What is your *why*? How many rounds of Twenty Questions have you played with God? I'll never know why autism exists or why my family was lucky enough to hit the genetic jackpot. And guess what? You'll never have the answers to your *whys* either.

> As the heavens are higher than the earth, so are my ways higher than your ways and my thoughts than your thoughts.
>
> Isaiah 55:9

Picture a carpenter ant crawling along a two-by-four. Now imagine trying to explain to that ant the glorious mansion the construction crew is erecting. This is how our narrow view of eternity prevents us from comprehending God's ways. When we try to make sense of God's plans, it's as if we grabbed our down comforter and barged into the throne room of heaven with Oreos caked in our teeth, screaming, "Move over buddy. That's my seat." The demand to know why doesn't bring freedom, but bondage. The whys of life become ropes which bind us, limiting what God can do in and through us.

I call this the Vicious Cycle of Pain.

Pain hits us, the pressure builds, and we experience the Great Undoing. If we choose to walk the path of Dwelling on the Why, we begin to question God's goodness and intentions for our life. Like he did to Adam and Eve, the serpent whispers in our ear, "Did God really say?" We snack on the fruit of the Tree of the Knowledge of Good and Evil and *we* determine what is best. We believe the lie that God can't be trusted. He isn't safe. He isn't good. He doesn't have our best interests in mind.

And guess what we will never do? Step out in faith. Why? We conclude that the same God who deserted us in our pain will surely abandon us if we risk and obey his directives. When we allow this cycle to continue unchecked, our hearts grow hard.

> When you hear what I say, you will not understand. When you see what I do, you will not comprehend. For the hearts of these people are hardened.
>
> Matthew 13:14–15 NLT

Man, that's the last thing I want—to turn into Uncle Scrooge or the Grinch. Before we know it, we're shutting out the world and walking around with a heart two sizes too small. Pain builds a barricade around our hearts. Our love for others diminishes and our ability to hear God's voice wanes. And the greatest tragedy: the enemy robs us of the opportunity for God to display his power *through* us because of our refusal to step out in faith. This vicious cycle continues on repeat as the years roll by.

Dying to the Why

I wasted months wrestling with God. Yes, I said wrestling. When we resist surrender, we attempt to secure God in a chokehold and claim the victory.

Right hook. Jab. Knee to the stomach. *My* way, God. *My* will.

But guess what? God always wins.

Jacob wrestled all night with the angel of the Lord. He demanded that God bless him. When the morning came, the angel touched Jacob's hip, causing him to limp the rest of his days.[1] Some of us are wasting our lives feuding with an all-powerful God. The end result? We collapse on the mat in exhaustion, squandering precious time and energy.

But Jesus came to show us a better way. He lived in complete obedience to his Father. His death and resurrection forged a way for each of us to have a relationship with God. And if that wasn't enough—He sent his Holy Spirit to soften the soil of our hardened hearts.

> I tell you the truth, unless a kernel of wheat is planted in the soil and dies, it remains alone. But its death will produce many new kernels—a plentiful harvest of new lives.
>
> John 12:24 NLT

A grain of wheat has an outer shell called the bran. It protects the plant embryo. But once the kernel is planted, the pressure of the soil cracks this shell. The plant breaks forth and new life begins. The bran represents our stubborn will and hard hearts. Inside, the wheat germ—with all its potential—symbolizes the Holy Spirit. It's only when we allow the pressure of pain to break us that the Holy Spirit is able to flow *through* us. And the result? Our lives will bear much fruit.

The truth is that your ability to be used by God isn't based upon your *wholeness* but your *brokenness*. God desires to redeem the pressure pain creates—like a chisel in his hand—to soften our hearts.

The Great Undoing, in Actuality, Is the Great Qualifier

No one understood this backward truth better than King David. After committing adultery with Bathsheba, murdering her

103

husband, and losing his newborn son—David was undone. Yet God was *not done* with David. He transcribed these wise words:

> My sacrifice, O God, is a broken spirit; a broken and contrite heart you, God, will not despise.

> Psalm 51:17

So how do we reverse the vicious cycle of pain? Surrender. The answer is simple, but the application is difficult. Something inside us has to stop fighting. Imagine allowing the Holy Spirit to pin your shoulder to the mat while you cry, "Uncle."

Your ways God, not mine. Your plan, not mine. Your life, not mine.

Surrender starts the day we make the conscious choice to drop our seed into the ground and bury it. This one decision changes everything. It's like when you go swimming at a friend's house and the water is cold. First, you dip your toes in. Then you dangle your feet and sit on the edge. Eventually, you may slither down the ladder, wincing every step of the way. It feels like a long, slow death. This is how I spent most of my life: calculating every decision and wincing every step. But the day I surrendered my daughter to God, a freedom came rushing in as I ran across the deck and flung myself into the pool, yelling, "Cannonball!"

This moment may sound petrifying. I get it, I'm a recovering control freak. But control is an illusion. All of our efforts to avoid heartache will fail. All of our intricate plans to construct a safe and happy life will collapse. And when they do, we will find ourselves just like the seed that refused to go into the ground—alone. The life we truly desire is on the other side of the Great Undoing.

My husband once had a dream of a dirt road littered with objects that defined him. Out of nowhere, God's giant arm reached down from heaven and in one fell swoop cleared the road. Before him stood an empty path. He had no idea where the trail may lead. He had nothing familiar to cling to. Yet one thing *did* remain: the hand of his Father.

This is surrender.

I didn't arrive at this place overnight. God is a gentleman. He doesn't demand immediate submission. Sometimes all you are able to muster is one baby step. This tiny stride still counts as forward motion. Worshiping with my daughter was my first wobbly step.

> Our limp is no longer a sign of weakness, but rather a badge of surrender.

Will you welcome pain onto the property of your life? Will you sign the building permit and authorize the enemy to construct a callus of unbelief around your heart? Or will you allow the pressure of pain to crack open your soul as you raise your white flag?

Your will be done, God, not mine.

Our limp is no longer a sign of weakness, but rather a badge of surrender.

PRAY THIS: *Dear Jesus, forgive me for challenging you to a wrestling match. I'm sorry for all the years I demanded you do things my way. I'm terrified to release the reins of my life. Help me take one wobbly step of surrender toward you. Teach me how to drop my seed in the ground, grab my shovel, and walk away. I know I can't see it now, but I choose to believe you can take the most painful moments of my life and birth something beautiful.*

DO THIS: Grab a piece of paper and a small box. Pray and ask God what one thing you are holding on to. Maybe it's not one thing but ten. Write them all down and put the piece of paper in the box. Then grab a shovel and dig a small hole in your backyard. Drop the box inside and cover it with dirt. It says in the Bible that the natural things come before the spiritual things.[2] Think of this as a physical way of releasing control, and watch in amazement at the harvest a tiny seed of surrender can produce.

TO THE MOM WHO ADDS A DASH OF FAITH TO HER LIFE:

Jesus is not a condiment or a side order. No amount of yoga, positive thinking, or trips to the spa can transform you. Jesus is the Way, the Truth, and the Life. In order to experience his abundant life, you must exchange your life for his. This will require you to die. I know, it doesn't sound fun. Death hurts most when you fight it. But the minute you surrender and take your last breath, the pain disappears. Let Jesus teach you how to die well.

7

The Suction of Self

Jesus, lift my head

When the will of God crosses the will of man, somebody has to die.

—Addison Leitch

The spring my daughter was diagnosed with autism, I was also diagnosed with a disorder: poormeitis.

Never heard of it?

It's an extreme case of self-pity resulting from the belief God owes us an easy life. On average, one in three moms suffer from this ailment. Initial symptoms include excessive sleeping, headaches, mood swings, and dry throat as a result of complaining too much. If left unattended, poormeitis will progress, causing some women to stop attending church, self-isolate, and—in some extreme cases—lose their faith entirely.

When I was first diagnosed, the doctor suggested I spend more time doing things for myself. I vacationed in Hawaii, but when I flew home, my problems were right where I left them. I bought a new wardrobe. But the high died off an hour later. I returned from my shopping spree with an armful of clothes and realized I never go anywhere, so trendy sweaters and designer jeans seemed pointless.

Here was the real issue: I expected God to bless me after I surrendered to him. Instead, life got harder. Our school psychologist explained that my daughter with autism lived in her own little world, but no one informed me that my world would shrink too. I went from working full time, to working part time, to never leaving my house except for a weekly grocery run to Aldi. Parks were impossible. Restaurants were disastrous. Even inviting friends over for dinner was a challenge as Mara often experienced hour-long meltdowns. While my husband would chat with our guests at the table, I'd be locked away in a bedroom with my wailing daughter.

Why does everyone else's life seem easier?

Fix this, Jesus.

But God wasn't trying to fix my life—he was trying to persuade me to lay it down.

Why Self-Care Has Sidelined a Generation

Contrary to popular belief, bubble baths, manicures, and lattes won't solve our problems as moms. There is a reason the book *The Purpose Driven Life* has sold over fifty million copies.

We're starved for purpose.

We are desperate to know there is a meaning to our suffering.

But the world keeps spoon-feeding us self-care propaganda. It tastes good for a hot second, but it lacks the nourishment our souls crave.

The truth is, we don't need to be persuaded to put ourselves first. A Harvard study revealed that on average, 60 percent of our conversations involve talking about ourselves. If that wasn't bad enough, 80 percent of our posts on social media are self-focused. Why? Scientists have discovered that when we talk about ourselves, the pleasure center of our brain lights up like a Christmas tree on an MRI.[1] So in a sense, our brains are hard-wired to think about one thing: ourselves. That's why it's easy for the enemy to run us off the road and cause us to fall into a pit of self-pity.

While our minds may operate on autopilot, our hearts yearn for more than a life wrapped up in me, myself, and I.

> Do you not know that in a race all the runners run, but only one gets the prize? Run in such a way as to get the prize.
>
> 1 Corinthians 9:24

If life is a race, self-care is an aid station. An aid station is a small tent located along the course of a marathon. It's a place to rest, hydrate, or grab a bite to eat. Hear me when I say this: self-care is necessary. Without aid stations, a runner could never complete the race.

But I fear culture has made self-care the finish line rather than a pit stop.

And where did this lie come from?

Do you know it's impossible for the enemy to create anything? God is the Creator. All the devil can do is distort one of his truths. The twisted myth the enemy wants you to believe? That self-care is the end goal.

Imagine I'm running a marathon. Around mile three, I'm coaxed by the crowd to beeline to the nearest aid station. After all, a small blister was forming on my pinkie toe, and I deserved an ice-cold lemonade. After a back massage and a cup of soup, I'm ready to get back in the race. Yet the crowd persuades me to grab a power bar and rest a little longer.

Most of us spend our lives hanging out at the aid station.

Nothing exciting happens at the aid station.

Self-care is lame if it's the finish line.

How long are you going to hang out under a tent with the Gatorade and bandages? How many years have you wasted convincing yourself you need another time out?

If Paul was on the sidelines of your life, he would be screaming, "Run!"

Jesus preached the same counter-cultural message:

> Then Jesus said to his disciples, "If any of you wants to be my follower, you must give up your own way, take up your cross, and follow me."
>
> Matthew 16:24 NLT

The race Jesus registered for led him to a cross. Yet he sprinted toward the finish line despite the pain, suffering, and loss. The prize set before him propelled him forward. And what was the prize?

You.

Jesus modeled for us a life that lives and dies for others—despite the cost. He proclaimed, "There is no greater love than to lay down one's life for one's friends."[2]

The goal isn't self-care but self-denial.

The goal isn't self-care but self-denial. This journey to the finish line will require you to lay down your life for others.

Will it be hard? Ridiculously hard.

Will it be painful? Excruciating at times.

Will you want to quit? Almost every day.

Will it be worth it? Absolutely.

Your purpose is found in the race.

Pride Leaving

"I can't believe we're doing this," I admitted to my husband on the thirty-minute car ride to the graduation party.

"We can't hide away forever," Greg said.

"I know but we've tried like a hundred times, and it always ends in disaster."

We rode in silence with the Veggie Tales theme song playing on repeat in the background.

As we pulled into the driveway, everyone looked surprised to see us. We piled out of the car and unbuckled our two toddlers from their car seats. The scene resembled the lifting of the starting gate at the horse races.

And they're off.

Jer ran to the dessert table and Mara dashed toward the river.

"Tag, you're it." I tapped Greg on the shoulder and motioned for him to run after her. "This was your idea after all."

Greg took off his flip-flops and handed them to me. He sprinted after Mara, who was always five steps ahead. I turned my back and decided to enjoy having a conversation with another adult. But after thirty minutes, I started to worry. Finally, Greg trudged up the hill with Mara's dripping Velcro sneakers in one hand and her body flung over his shoulder. Her little fists beat his back and her bare feet kicked against his stomach. As he approached, Mara's ear-piercing scream drew the entire graduation party to attention.

"Party's over!" Greg yelled as he pulled the car keys from his pocket, making sure not to look anyone in the eyes as he passed. I apologized to the host, grabbed my son's hand, and headed to the car.

This scene happened over and over again. The details were different, but the outcome was always the same. Later that night, I called my mom to vent.

"It was so embarrassing, Mom."

"I know, honey, but it's a good thing. Whenever you feel that sting, pride is leaving. When pride leaves, there's a little bit less of you and a little bit more of Jesus."

Jesus' Favorite Camping Spot

The conversation with my mom felt like a crack of light shining through a door that was once slammed in my face. When God doesn't change our *circumstances*, he wants to change our *perspective*. When we hyper-focus on ourselves, suffering feels pointless. And when suffering feels pointless, life feels hopeless. But let me plant in your heart a mustard seed of faith today. What if God desires to use this hard season to mold you into the person he created you to be? Maybe your pain could serve a purpose.

> And we know that all that happens to us is working for our good if we love God and are fitting into his plans.
>
> Romans 8:28 TLB

God can morph the most horrendous circumstances of our lives into something beautiful. But there are two conditions in this verse. All things that happen to us are working for our good *if* we love God. This promise is for the Christian. Life can feel like one trauma on top of another—suicide, divorce, cancer, death. Many of these scenarios have no happy endings or good outcomes. But for the Christian, God promises to flip the script and redeem that which was been stolen.

The second condition? All that happens to us is working for our good *if* we love God *and* are fitting into his plans. We can't twist God's arm and fit him into *our* five-year plan. This requires us to rip up our vision boards and start praying bold prayers:

Your way, God, not mine.

Your will, not mine.

Your story, not mine.

I found myself on a journey with special needs parenting I never intended to take. But Jesus' favorite spot to set up camp is the gap between the life you envisioned and the one you now live. We need to get comfortable living in the tension of what *we thought* and what *God intended*. For the surrendered Christian, this is home.

Paul speaks of this when he compares walking in the Spirit versus walking in the flesh. Our flesh wants things our way. But as children of God, we have the privilege of sharing in Jesus' suffering, so that we may also share in his glory.[3] How much courage would we possess if we dared to believe God can use *anything* the enemy throws at us for his glory and our good?

> Jesus' favorite spot to set up camp is the gap between the life you envisioned and the one you now live.

Listen to me. You didn't miss God's will for your life.

It just looks radically different than what you imagined.

Trust the process.

The Best Advice

When my daughter was first diagnosed, I didn't know a single parent raising a child with autism. I attended one meeting at an autism support group and left in tears. The spectrum is so wide. At the meeting, a parent shared how her son didn't have any friends. Another mom talked about how her daughter was unable to tie her shoes. This meeting confirmed that Mara was far worse than any of the kids represented in that room. I wanted to stand up and yell, "Do any of your kids smear poop all over the walls? Do they leave holes in your sheetrock? Do you know what it feels like to care for a child who never says 'Mommy' or 'I love you'?"

I sought the support group as triage, but instead, I found myself bleeding out the entire walk to my car. I vowed to never go back.

A few days later, I approached the missions pastor at our church. She wasn't a special needs parent, but her life had been far from easy. Her husband was diagnosed with AIDS in the eighties. They lived in Bermuda at the time, and there was little to no care because of the stigma surrounding the disease. While raising her two young sons, she cared for her husband in their home until he died. This was followed by a dark season of her soul, where depression tried to swallow her whole. Yet somehow, she healed from this trauma and was still investing her life into others.

"How did you do it, Christine?" I asked.

"When I was at my lowest, my mom told me something that changed everything. 'Find someone in a worse spot and help them.' You have to get your eyes off yourself. It's that simple."

After Christine's husband passed, she opened a home to care for others suffering with AIDS. She offered her patients the dignity and love the medical community had denied them. Her ministry led her in later years to travel to Uganda for a Christian event. While driving in the bush, Christine came across dozens of children working in a rock quarry. Each wore nothing more than an oversized t-shirt as they crouched under the blazing African sun. For twelve hours a day, these kids chipped rocks into gravel with a homemade hammer. The goal? To fill three buckets. The payment for their labor? Eighteen cents.

When Christine returned to Bermuda, the scene was seared into her memory.

"I had to do something," she explained.

This encounter led Christine to travel to Uganda many times and open a children's home. This home housed fifteen children whose tummies were filled and schooling was paid, and who learned about the love of Jesus. Eventually, our church would take over this ministry, and to this day, we are loving on these kids, who are now young adults.

All because one woman decided to *look up* from her pain and *look out* at a broken world.

Jesus Rummaging in My Hall Closet

Christine's words inspired me. But I couldn't abandon my family, hop on a plane, and fly to Africa. What could *I* do to get my eyes off myself?

As I was complaining, God interrupted my rant mid-sentence with a thought.

What is one thing *you can do now that you couldn't do before?*

"Nothing," I yelled. "I can't even leave my house, Jesus."

That question marinated in my heart for a week. I imagined Jesus ringing my doorbell. I welcomed him in, but he brushed past me without a word. He headed over to my hall closet and started pulling stuff out.

"Jesus, what are you doing?" I asked.

No answer.

Fifteen minutes passed. Junk filled my hallway, and I was ashamed of the mess. Jesus was exposing all the stuff I'd shoved behind closed doors for years.

"Ah-ha! Here it is," Jesus said as he pulled out an old journal and blew the dust off the cover. He flipped through the pages and pointed to my journal entry that read "When I get older, I want to adopt."

That's the one thing.

Maybe I watched one too many Hallmark movies as a teen, but I always envisioned myself adopting an African American boy. Yet life has a way of shoveling loads of dirt on top of our God dreams. Despite the limited life I was given, what if God was about to resurrect a dream I forgot existed?

Maybe, just maybe, there was a purpose to my pain.

The Suction of Self

Self-pity is self-worship in disguise. It takes our eyes off God and places the focus on ourselves. It reminds me of the plant in the

117

musical *The Little Shop of Horrors*. If you've never seen the Broadway show, track with me for a minute. A flower shop assistant named Seymour discovers an unusual plant that resembles a talking Venus flytrap. (I know, it's weird.) The plant is demanding, yelling, "Feed me, Seymour." The only problem? He doesn't want plant food. His favorite snack is human blood. The more the plant eats, the bigger he becomes, until he is so massive that he's unstoppable. The same is true when we feed our flesh. When we walk in the flesh, we continually need to keep feeding ourselves.

What we feed grows. And as our flesh grows, it becomes more demanding, until one day we realize we've created a monster.

> Self-pity is self-worship in disguise. It takes our eyes off God and places the focus on ourselves.

Look at me.

Feel sorry for me.

See how bad my problems are.

When we operate in self-pity, we don't want answers, we want attention. It sucks the life out of ourselves and our loved ones. People avoid us when we walk into a room. It may be subconscious, but a part of us is screaming, "Feed me!" As friends and family pull away, it confirms the lie we believed all along—we're alone. The enemy wants us to live in the pit of self-pity, isolating us from a world that needs us and a God who loves us.

Self-help touts, "Me first," while Jesus taught, "God first."

Positioning God first is like buttoning a dress shirt. Line up the top button, and everything else falls into place.

God created you for greater things than yourself.

All you have to do is look up.

The Phone Call That Changed Everything

I googled the phone number for Social Services and then stared at my computer screen for fifteen minutes. I picked up the phone and set it back down. I dialed and hung up—twice.

What if I don't love the children I adopt as much as I love my own?
What if I neglect my family in order to care for someone else's?
What if, what if, what if.

Foster care is like a polar plunge fundraiser. Foster parents are the lunatics who dash toward the ice-cold river in the middle of winter while everyone else hangs out on the shore, shaking their heads in disbelief.

It's a shock to your system. It's a leap of faith and the world stands in awe at your audacity. My husband and I were on the same page. But my family thought I should be checked into a mental hospital.

"Why would you want to adopt? You have too much on your plate already," my mom said.

"Because Jesus told me to."

"It doesn't make sense. You should be focusing on Mara," she advised.

But that's the thing; following the Holy Spirit doesn't make sense.

Am I suggesting every parent should adopt?

Absolutely not.

But I want you to imagine Jesus showing up at your door and rummaging through your hall closet. When he's finished, he asks you two questions:

1. How can you get your eyes off yourself?
2. What is *one thing* you can do now that you couldn't do before?

I don't care how limited your life may feel. If you answer these two questions, God can use the hard seasons of your life to change you from the inside out. Your pain can serve a purpose.

Greg and I enrolled in a ten-week course to become certified foster parents. We laughed. We cried. We were scared out of our minds. We talked about quitting before we even finished the course.

Then we got the call that changed everything.

My cell rang and I recognized the number: the Department of Social Services. A call from them was terrifying and thrilling at the same time. They asked us to foster a newborn baby girl. I contacted my husband to run the placement by him and rushed to the hospital to pick her up. When I rounded the corner, I ran into the case worker. She informed me there had been a miscommunication.

"Intake told me the baby was a girl. But actually—"

I strained to read her clipboard as we headed toward the maternity ward. But when I looked up, I whipped my arm across the case worker's chest. It was as if we were in a car accident, and I was protecting her from the oncoming crash. In that moment, my heart suffered a head-on collision with the most perfect African American baby boy swaddled behind the nursery glass. The same boy I had dreamt of my entire life.

God penned the purposes and plans for our lives before time began.[4] All we have to do is get our eyes off ourselves and look up.

PRAY THIS: *Dear Jesus, forgive me for falling into the pit of self-pity. I don't want to be stuck in this hole forever. It's hard to look up when I'm hurting. Sometimes I feel so alone and it seems like no one cares. I choose to focus on you and your love. Only you can pull me out of this pit. I want to walk by faith, but in order to do so, I must keep my eyes locked on you. It's not about me. It's all about you. Help me to believe you have more for me to do.*

DO THIS: Imagine Jesus showing up at your door and rummaging through your hall closet. When he's finished, he asks you two questions:

1. How can you get your eyes off yourself?
2. What is *one thing* you can do now that you couldn't do before?

TO THE MOM STRETCHED THIN:

*I know you feel pulled
in every direction,
but growth is found
in the stretch.*

8

The Comfort Zone

Jesus, stretch my faith

God doesn't call us to be comfortable. He calls us to trust Him
so completely that we are unafraid to put ourselves in situations
where we will be in trouble if He doesn't come through.

—Francis Chan, *Crazy Love*

When I was a kid, the hot item on everyone's Christmas list was
a doll named Stretch Armstrong. He was a wrestler whose arms
and legs were constructed of a rubbery material that could stretch
across our entire living room, and when we let go, he would snap
right back into place.

Most days, I feel like Stretch Momstrong—pulled in a million
directions—except I don't snap back into place. The stretch of life
has left me saggy, like the flap of skin on my tummy after having
one too many babies. Nothing impressive to see here.

Life has a way of stretching us to the point of snapping.

My husband and I transported our foster son to visits with his biological parents seven days a week. Our house was a revolving door for case workers, Social Services, and early intervention teachers. Juggling the needs of my daughter on the spectrum along with court dates, doctor appointments, and enough paperwork to cover the Atlantic in origami swans stretched me to the max. There weren't enough hours in the day to complete it all. I was sure I was failing as a mother, as a foster parent, and as a Christian. Whenever I complained, my mom would flash me the I-told-you-so look.

To top things off, a week into fostering Isaac, I found myself in the bathroom staring at a positive pregnancy test.

Really, God?

Stretch Momstrong is gonna snap.

I'm sure you've felt the stretch. We orchestrate our whole lives trying to avoid it.

If it's uncomfortable, it can't be God, right?

But growth is found in the stretch. Without the pull, God can never enlarge our capacity to carry and birth his purposes into this world.

Growing Pains

"Five foot, six inches," the nurse said, scribbling it down on her chart.

"I'm five-seven. I've been five-seven since I was sixteen years old. Want to see my driver's license?" I demanded while rummaging through my purse.

Refusing my documentation, the nurse obliged to measure me one more time.

"Five foot, six inches on the dot. Sometimes people shrink, my dear."

I rolled my eyes, writing the poor lady off as incompetent. Even though I'm still in denial, the human body reaches its maximum height when we hit twenty years old.[1] Our skeletal systems finish growing by the time we can legally drink our first margarita.

Inevitably, we stop growing and start shrinking.

Our mind, on the other hand, continues to mature. Scientists have discovered our brains reach full maturity around the age of twenty-five.[2] I once heard a high school graduation speech where the principal informed the seniors it was acceptable for them to make impulsive decisions. Why? Because the prefrontal cortex of their brain was not fully developed yet. (News flash: Teenagers don't need our permission to do stupid things.) All the parents—including myself—wanted to boo her off the stage.

Eventually, our physical bodies cease to grow (height-wise; width-wise may be a different story). Our minds stop maturing. But what about our spirits? If the Holy Spirit lives within us—we should have unlimited potential.

Yet when was the last time you tossed and turned at night with spiritual growing pains? When was the last time you ran into someone you hadn't seen in a while and they stopped you mid-sentence to say, "Wow. I don't even recognize you. Your faith has grown so much."

Paul implored Timothy from a Roman prison to "fan into flame the gift of God."[3]

Paul saw Timothy's potential.

Timothy saw his limits.

Yet Paul knew a secret—Christians need a fan. The flickering embers of your first love will die out unless you fan them into flames. When my family builds a campfire, we don't blow on the fire to get it going. We are go-big-or-go-home people. My husband pulls out the leaf blower and pummels that thing with O_2 whenever the fire starts to die down.

What about you? There used to be something in you that burned for God. A gift inside of you that is dying to be released into the world. A melody only you can sing.

But slow-burning coals die out. You must grab the leaf blower and go to town.

Why?

Because without intentionality, we wander.

Here lies the problem: making a decision for Jesus occurs on an exact date, in a definitive location, at a specific moment in time, and is purely a conscious choice. But falling away from Jesus—oh man, that's quite the opposite. It occurs gradually, over a long period of time, at a snail's pace, and it is largely an unconscious choice. There is no status quo in Christianity. If we aren't rowing our hearts out, we will drift further and further from the human God envisioned when he gathered a lump of clay with you on his mind.

Growing pains suck.

Sometimes they hurt.

Sometimes you look awkward and gangly when you walk.

Sometimes people laugh at your baby steps of faith.

But as you grow, it's as if God reaches down from heaven and cranks the volume knob on your life, exclaiming, "Turn her up. I love this song."

Kiddy Chairs and Wheelbarrows

I waddled into the children's section of the library with the car seat locked in the crook of my arm. I waved at the case worker perched on the end of a yellow kiddy chair two sizes too small. Setting the car seat on the table next to her, I plopped down in my own tiny chair with a sigh.

"You look tired," she said.

"I'm exhausted. I didn't sleep at all last night," I admitted while rubbing my pregnant belly. "Where's Isaac's mom?"

"She's in the restroom. She isn't feeling well—morning sickness," the case worker explained.

I almost fell out of my tiny chair.

"What did you say?"

"Never mind," the case worker said as her face went flush. Apparently, I was the only one who didn't get the memo.

Sure enough, six months after I gave birth to my son Jacob, we received a call from Social Services asking us if Isaac's baby sister could be placed in our home. In a matter of thirteen months, we found ourselves with three babies all under the age of two.

There is a reason triplets are a rare anomaly. Moms weren't created to be spread this thin. Two kids, my husband and I could wrangle. But five kids—one on the severe end of the spectrum and three babies—was a rodeo, and we found ourselves trampled on, face-first in the mud. What bothered me most was that it appeared my steps of obedience led me to this place.

I once heard an analogy about faith that stuck with me. Imagine God owns a wheelbarrow and a pair of Carhartt overalls. Envision God and his wheelbarrow balancing on a tightrope that stretches the entire expanse of Niagara Falls. As God is about to cross, he asks you to hop in.

"Trust me," he says. "I've done this before."

Would you jump in? Or would it be a hard pass? When was the last time you put yourself in a position where if God didn't come through, you'd be in big trouble? This is the stretch of faith. Fear shrinks God, and with a God that small we scramble to help him. Faith magnifies God, and with a God that big we can rest knowing he's got this.

I don't know your situation, but listen to me, God has got you.

The God who spins the earth at the exact rotational speed to sustain life is the same God who orders your steps. The God who created, rules, and reigns over two trillion galaxies is the same God watching over your children. The God who designed the intricate complexity of the DNA molecule is the same God who is aware of every unseen burden you carry.

> Faith magnifies God, and with a God that big we can rest knowing he's got this.

The God who dresses billions of lilies and cares for the smallest of birds is the same God who promises to provide for all your needs. And the God who sacrificed his only son to have a relationship with you is the same God who will do anything to win your love.

Stop magnifying your problems. Start magnifying God.

The safest place you can be is in the center of his wheelbarrow.

Stretching Tent Pegs

With five kiddos under one roof, I started concocting plans to escape my house. My go-to's were running and coffee—not at the same time. That would be disastrous. One afternoon, I grabbed a latte with a friend and found myself complaining about being stretched thin.

"I love you, Jess, but you did this to yourself," she said.

Her words were a punch in the gut. I *did* do this to myself. I said yes to fostering because I felt God told me to. We said yes to having more biological children because we didn't want to live in fear. We said yes when Social Services called to place Isaac's baby sister in our home. My husband and I made these choices; no one twisted our arms. Each decision was bathed in prayer and birthed from a place of obedience.

> "Sing, barren woman, you who never bore a child;
> burst into song, shout for joy, you who were never in labor;
> because more are the children of the desolate woman
> than of her who has a husband," says the Lord.
>
> Isaiah 54:1

For seventy years the Jewish people were held captive by the Babylonians. Many never knew any other life. So when King Cyrus declared the Israelites could return to Jerusalem and rebuild the city, most stayed put.

Comfort was their king.

Do you know you can grow comfortable anywhere—even in the enemy's camp—if you remain there long enough?

God anticipated their stubbornness and delivered a prophetic word to propel his people forward. Sometimes we need a good shove from God. The prophet compares the Israelites to a woman unable to conceive. In the Jewish culture, a barren woman was looked upon as a disgrace. But God promised the shame of their captivity would be a distant memory. Soon they would be freaking out like a mom who discovers a plus sign on her pregnancy test. But in order to see this promise fulfilled, they had to do one thing: stretch.

> Enlarge the place of your tent, stretch your tent curtains
>   wide, do not hold back;
> lengthen your cords, strengthen your stakes.
> For you will spread out to the right and to the left;
>   your descendants will dispossess nations and settle in
>   their desolate cities.
>
> Isaiah 54:2–3

God promised the Israelites would grow in number and would need to expand their living space. The prophet used the analogy of a tent because as exiles, the Israelites had been living in tents for the last seventy years. But despite this great word of increase, only 50,000 Jews traveled the nine hundred miles back to Israel. The rest remained in Babylon.

Why?

Because our flesh hates the stretch.

But if we don't embrace the uncomfortable, God can never expand our hearts and influence. Lengthening the cords of our lives represents our reach, while strengthening the stakes represents the depth of our relationship with God. We can't expand and do all God calls us to do if we don't intentionally put ourselves in situations that stretch us. Faith isn't merely a stagnant belief in God and his power—faith *is* the stretch. We must be like the woman with the issue of blood. She believed with childlike faith that her healing was only an arm's length away. She pushed through the crowd and grabbed the hem of Jesus' robe and was instantly healed. Jesus' robe didn't heal her, the *stretch* did.[4]

Faith isn't merely a stagnant belief in God and his power— faith IS the stretch.

Do you know that if you trap a flea in a glass jar with a lid for a few days and then remove the cap, the flea will only jump to where the lid once was? He will have grown accustomed to his limited environment and will spend the rest of his short life in that dang jar—even though he's free.

Is the job you've worked for the last ten years what Jesus is calling you to do now? Are your friendships propelling you upward toward the things of God or dragging you down? Are old mindsets preventing you from stepping out in faith? Do you see yourself as just a mom or more than a conqueror?

Paul felt so strongly about our victory in Christ, he made up a word when he called the Roman believers super conquerors. Yet most of us look in the mirror and see a barely-getting-by loser. Victory is not based on what *you've* done, but on what *Jesus* did. And from this place of triumph, we stretch out in radical, audacious ways and watch in amazement at what God will do in and through us.

Stretched Not Stressed

It's easy to read this chapter and conclude that in order to grow in faith we must stretch ourselves thin as Christians. But that is not the case. Jesus isn't calling us to be super moms, with our calendars booked and our hands in everything. It's less about overextending ourselves and more about extending our hand to Jesus and expanding our reliance on him.

What is the one thing God has laid on your heart to do that will stretch your faith?

Obedience is better than sacrifice.[5] I know it's terrifying to climb into a wheelbarrow as you peer over the edge at the colossal falls below, but we only have two choices.

1. We can shrink back and remain on the cliff of comfort with the enemy's stamp of approval.
2. We can stretch out in obedience with the Father's protection, Jesus' blessing, and the Holy Spirit's power.

Either way, we'll want to pee our pants. But only obedience takes us where we could never go ourselves.

The Stretch Makes Us Weak

After my daughter was born, I broke free from the house a few days a week for a twenty-minute jog. After the foster babies arrived and I gave birth to my son Jacob, I realized I needed *more* time alone. My twenty-minute runs turned into forty, then an hour, then two hours, then three. The only logical way to increase my time out of the house was to increase the number of miles I ran. Honestly, I walked many of those miles while staring at nature and blasting worship music in my AirPods. But I became infatuated with running. Running offered me the space to be me. No diapers, no phone calls, no whining, and no one to interrupt me—just my thoughts and God's presence.

I decided to register for a trail run through the mountains of Pennsylvania. When I think of a trail, I imagine a well-manicured bike path buzzing with dog owners and gray-haired speed walkers. Instead, I found myself in the middle of a forest in the pitch-dark reciting *lions, tigers, and bears—oh my* on repeat in my head.

"What the heck am I doing?" I asked my husband as I stood in a pack of experienced runners decked out in their Camelbak hydration packs, caked in anti-chafing body cream.

131

"You're going to do great," Greg said while glancing down at my shaking legs. "Are you cold?"

"No, I'm scared out of my mind."

After I spent an hour pacing back and forth and praying I wasn't eaten by a bear, the gun went off. The course traveled through steep mountainsides, down deep ravines, and up onto flat country roads. At one point, I had to cross a rope traverse over a stream. Halfway through my run, as I was jogging on a dirt road, I heard a pop in my knee.

That can't be good.

I hobbled to the side of the trail to assess the damage. My shin and knee looked fine, but every time I took a step, a sharp shooting pain launched up my calf. Due to the strain of the run, the fibers of my tendon had overstretched, causing a partial tear.

Eventually my husband, who was trailing behind me in our Honda Pilot, pulled over and rolled down his window.

"Why did you stop?"

"I tore something in my knee," I said with my head hanging low.

"Can you walk?" Greg asked.

"Yeah, but that will take forever."

"Who cares? You're only racing against yourself. Push through the pain. You've got this," Greg said as he grabbed a handful of salted cashews and threw them in his mouth.

I don't know how, but I finished that race. The grace of God carried me. Each step was like the twist of a corkscrew lodged in my kneecap. I couldn't fathom making it to the end and surviving to tell the tale. I didn't have much faith. But here is the good news: God doesn't require us to have faith for the future, just faith for one more step. It's not a leap or a journey—it's a walk—one step at a time.

When I reached the last mile, I sprinted uphill. I forgot the discomfort of each wincing step and relished the moment. As the crowds came into view, I recognized my husband's voice cheering me on. And when I crossed that finish line, every painful step was oh, so worth it.

Bragging about Our Weakness

We tend to avoid anything that stretches our faith because it hurts. And pain is a constant reminder that we are weak and pathetic. The apostle Paul referred to a thorn in his flesh. Bible scholars aren't sure if Paul was blind. But they are certain that he struggled with a physical ailment that was a severe limitation. Yet Paul never let it hold him back. Rather than complain about his weakness, Paul bragged about it:

> Three times I pleaded with the Lord to take it away from me. But he said to me, "My grace is sufficient for you, for my power is made perfect in weakness." Therefore I will boast all the more gladly about my weaknesses, so that Christ's power may rest on me. That is why, for Christ's sake, I delight in weaknesses, in insults, in hardships, in persecutions, in difficulties. For when I am weak, then I am strong.
>
> 2 Corinthians 12:8–10

Our weakness is a permission slip for God to show off in our lives. He refuses to display his power when our world is neat and put together. But the Holy Spirit delights to make an appearance when our lives are stretched. Motherhood and all its demands create the perfect conditions for God to strut his stuff. But he waits for us to humbly send the invitation. We must drop the facade and learn to brag about all the ways we fall short.

Where our limits end—his unlimited power begins.

When we feel incapable—his supernatural strength is on display.

When we are weak—he is strong.

In the movie *Forrest Gump*, there is a scene where Forrest is running with braces on his legs. He makes a mad dash from a bunch of bullies and as he runs, the movie switches to slow motion. At first, his run is gangly and awkward, but slowly he finds his stride, and the braces fall off. Listen to me: what once hindered you from running after God will fall to the wayside if you just keep running. "Run, Forrest, run!"

On December 17, 2014, Isaac and Emma officially joined the Hurlbut clan. Along with my salvation, adoption is hands-down one of the best decisions of my life. Every visit, every meeting, every form we filled out felt microscopic compared to the glorious celebration that ensued on Gotcha Day.

> Our weakness is a permission slip for God to show off in our lives.

When we get to heaven one day, we aren't going to think, "Man, I wish I would have watched more Netflix." Rather, the growing pains and stretch marks we experience on earth will pale in comparison to the eternal rewards that await us. It's the same way a pregnant mom feels after giving birth. Her pain is eclipsed by joy the second her healthy baby is placed in her arms.

Push through the pain.

Embrace the stretch.

Because one day when we reach our heavenly finish line with the cloud of witnesses cheering us on—it will be oh, so worth it.

PRAY THIS: *Dear Jesus, forgive me for wanting comfort more than I want you. I know the only way my faith can grow is in the stretch. I believe you're with me, Jesus, but help my unbelief. I'm sorry for all the times I have complained about how hard my life is. Rather than grumble about my circumstances, teach me to brag about my weaknesses, because I know that's your favorite place to show up.*

DO THIS: What is the one thing God has laid on your heart to do that will stretch your faith? Spend some time in prayer and ask God. Maybe you already know the answer. Then take one practical step this week in that direction. Climb into his wheelbarrow and trust your Dad has got you.

TO THE MOM TRAPPED AT HOME:

I know you feel like the invisible man. But you're always on Jesus' mind, and your name is engraved in the halls of heaven. Your hidden years are never wasted years.

9

The Heaviness of Hiddenness

Jesus, remember me

In seasons of hiddenness our sense of value is disrupted, stripped of what "others" affirmed us to be. In this season God intends to give us an unshakable identity in Him, that no amount of adoration nor rejection can alter.

—Alicia Britt Chole, *Anonymous*

I always thought panic attacks weren't a real thing—until I experienced my first one.

The morning started like any other. Isaac was up before the sun, crouched on the floor beside our bed, gawking at me until I opened my eyes.

"Isaac, what are you doing?"

"Elmo's World?" he asked sheepishly.

I stumbled out of bed and wandered into the living room to discover my daughter Mara was also awake, rummaging through the fridge.

"You guys, it's six a.m.," I snapped.

First order of business: Operation Diaper Change. I had it down to a science: first Isaac, then Emma, then Jacob. I handed a pull-up to Mara.

"Go potty. The bus is coming."

"No-no school," Mara stammered.

"We have school today."

I picked out an outfit and yanked it over her head as she pulled away.

"No school," she repeated.

She squeezed my forearms, which was a common response when things didn't go Mara's way. I pulled out a hairbrush from the vanity drawer.

"Mommy will be gentle."

Mara hit the brush out of my hand, and it landed in the bathroom sink and spun around.

"Mara Grace," I yelled while catching a glance of the bus out our front window.

"The bus is here. Forget your hair," I said while I slipped on her book bag and nudged her out of the house. Mara shuffled her feet and covered her ears. The bus door closed, and I waved goodbye.

God, help her day go smoothly.

But as I headed back inside, a horn startled me. I turned and the driver motioned.

"Mara is refusing to sit in her seat. Can you help?"

I climbed aboard the bus and discovered Mara like a cork in a bottle's neck—lodged in the aisle—ready to pop.

"Mara, you have to buckle up."

"No school."

I scooped her up and sat her on the bench. Pressing Mara's hips into the seat, I fought to buckle her in as she kicked my shins and screamed in my face. A part of me wanted to kick her back.

What mom wants to kick her own child?

"No school! No school!"

In the middle of this ordeal, my front door swung open as Isaac tottered out. He chuckled as his bare feet crunched under the snow.

Are you serious?

A toddler entourage followed. Emma and Jacob waddled toward the road while our dog ran in circles around the bus barking, alerting me of my escapees.

The chaos never stops. It never ends.

I dragged Mara off the bus, rallied my troops into the house one by one, and locked the door from the inside.

My tears turned into sobs.

My sobs morphed into hyperventilating and before I knew it—I was having my first panic attack. I called my husband and tried to convey what happened, but I couldn't catch my breath to get the words out. Leaning against our kitchen wall, I hung up mid-sentence and slid down to the worn linoleum floor and collapsed, bawling uncontrollably for thirty minutes.

Maybe you've been there. The circumstances of your life may be different, but the overwhelming feeling of exhaustion coupled with complete loss of control is universal.

The chaos never stops. It never ends.

The whole bus scene felt like a microcosm of my life. A tornado of chaos swirled around me—threatening the safety of me and my kids—yet *nobody* could help me. I had to be everything to everyone. The weight of this responsibility felt like a 250-pound python lying on my chest, coiling around my body, and choking the life out of me.

A God Who Sees

I jolted to my feet when I heard a thud coming from the living room. Wiping my snotty nose with the sleeve of my sweatshirt, I dashed to the rescue.

I don't have time to cry.

Emma had knocked over a lamp and it was dangling by the cord. I set it back and tapped my daughter's hand.

"No touching."

I took a deep breath and walked over to the sink to tackle the dishes. When I'm sad, I clean. When I'm angry, I clean. When I'm depressed, I clean. Somehow, the order of a room makes the madness of my life more bearable. It's one thing I can control. Scrubbing a pot with a Brillo pad a little too hard, I found myself staring out the window above the sink. Mesmerized by a robin braving the cold, I watched as he chirped and swooped from branch to branch in the maple tree next to our garage. This one thought paralyzed me:

He looks so free and I'm a prisoner in my own home.

I can't explain what happened next. I wasn't praying. I wasn't even thinking about God. But as I gazed out my window, it felt as if I heard the audible voice of Jesus. It was so vivid, I turned to see if someone had walked into the room.

He spoke three words to my heart that changed everything: "I see you."

A wave of emotion crashed over me, but these tears were different. Instead of feeling alone—I felt seen. Known. Loved.

I caught a glimpse of the One who sees me.

And he sees *you* too.

Giving Names to God

For eight years, I was a shut-in. Scrolling through Instagram, I had a front row seat as my friends and their families enjoyed the summer. They hopped on planes sporting mouse ears, turned into lobsters boating on the river, and stuffed their faces with s'mores on weekend camping trips.

Meanwhile, I sat alone trapped in my home.

Hiddenness looks different. Sometimes it comes in the form of caring for an aging parent or spouse. The silence is deafening.

Other times, it's brimming with dirty diapers, fingerprints plastered on windows, and the pitter-patter of little feet. The noise is maddening. There are seasons when our health fails and our very own bodies become the prison cells that confine us.

No matter what your circumstance, we all experience seasons where we are trapped inside staring out at a world passing us by.

Do you know there was only one person in the Bible who had the honor of giving God a name? And she was the least likely candidate. Hagar was an Egyptian slave and a single mom on the run. Sarai, Abram's wife, was unable to have children. God appeared to Abram and promised him his descendants would be more than the stars in the sky. Years passed, and Sarai got tired of waiting and took matters into her own hands. She demanded Abram sleep with Hagar as a means to grow a family through her womb. But once Hagar became pregnant, a jealous spirit rose within Sarai. Things got so bad, Hagar ran away. She found herself in her own hidden season, alone in the wilderness with no food, no money, and no one to care for her. While she rested at a spring, the Lord appeared to her, stating he had heard her cry.

When no one heard, God was listening.

When no one cared, God showed up.

And when no one saw, God took notice.

At that moment, Hagar gave God a name: El Roi.

"You are the God who sees me," for she said, "I have now seen the One who sees me."

Genesis 16:13

If you find yourself serving a house arrest sentence you don't deserve, remember, God sees you. He sees you performing double duty: showering, bathing, brushing, and dressing, not only yourself but your loved ones. It's easy to question your life's purpose when every day feels like Groundhog Day. But know this: God records every selfless act of love in his *Book of Remembrance*.

Every small deed is monumental in his eyes. And what you have done behind closed doors will one day be rewarded openly. Because in the end, you will discover you weren't just caring for your child—but for Jesus himself.

> Truly I tell you, whatever you did for one of the least of these brothers and sisters of mine, you did for me.

> Matthew 25:40

Hidden Things

I felt a peace knowing God took notice of me during my hidden years, but I still struggled with a spirit of shame I couldn't shake. Like the cloud of dust that encircled the Peanut's character Pig-pen, it followed me wherever I went. I was a player called to sit the bench. I was a child in timeout with my nose pressed into a corner. It doesn't make sense, but I felt like God was embarrassed of me.

I think my shame stemmed from childhood. You see, I grew up in the nineties. I wore my overalls with one strap down. I memorized the entire opening of "The Fresh Prince of Bel-Air." My bookshelves were lined with trolls, and I sported a poodle perm that made my head the shape of a perfect triangle. But the greatest tragedy of this decade was self-inflicted: my over-plucked eyebrows. One afternoon, I stole my mom's tweezers, locked myself in the bathroom, climbed on top of the sink to get a closer look, and went to town on my beautiful brows until they were pencil thin. My big brows weren't my only blessing. God also gifted me with a large forehead and long nose, which were only exaggerated when my eyebrows no longer existed.

I strutted into first period believing I looked like Drew Barrymore until several people gasped as they passed me in the hall. I intended to burn my school picture, but my mom discovered it in my backpack, framed it, and hung it in our entryway. At one point, I grabbed a pen and tried to draw my eyebrows back on.

My husband has never seen this photo. It's buried in a box in our basement, never to see the light of day.

We tend to hide things we're ashamed of.

The old journal, the bad report card, the wedding ring after the divorce is final.

So when God called *me* into a season of hiddenness, I snatched my cloak of shame and draped it over my shoulders—because I was sure people hid things they were embarrassed by.

Human Hearts in Treasure Chests

During my hidden season, Jesus reminded me of a Valentine's Day gift an old boyfriend gave me. It was a creepy replica of a human heart he made in ceramics class. It was meant to be sentimental. But it was so realistic—complete with arteries, veins, and an aorta—it felt more like something out of a Wes Craven horror movie. He set his creation in a decorative box with a secret compartment underneath which housed a time capsule. Inside were notes folded into triangles, old photos, and weird mementos we shared, like paperclip necklaces.

There is another reason people hide things: because they can't put a price tag on them. Some of the most valuable things in this world are hidden away under lock and key. And maybe—just maybe—it's the hidden ones God wants all to himself.

Listen to me, no matter how invisible you feel or how many years have passed—you're not forgotten. God is not ashamed of you, angry at you, or embarrassed by you. He's proud to be seen with you. You are invaluable to him. If God desires to hide you away for a season, it will only make your reveal that much more glorious.

The truth is, God is in the hiding business. But what is the purpose of our hidden seasons? God may not have a Get Out of Jail Free card waiting for you this lap around the board, but there is value in hidden things. Over the last eight years, God has revealed these beautiful truths to me:

1. Hidden Things Grow

Jesus spent thirty years in obscurity—living in his parents' basement—and three years ministering. Those numbers are a tad disproportionate to me. He didn't seem to be in a rush to save the world. He never felt the urge to prove his worth or exploit his power. Jesus couldn't care less about establishing a name or building a following. He was content to remain anonymous until his appointed time.

> If God desires to hide you away for a season, it will only make your reveal that much more glorious.

Why would God's Son spend three decades crafting dining room tables in Joseph's wood shop?

Isolated.

Alone.

Working remotely.

Wouldn't he have been more productive investing his time preaching, teaching, and healing the sick? But Jesus wasn't worried about being productive. He was more concerned with being obedient.

Jesus came to the world to model for us a better way to live. He did what he saw his Father do. He said what he heard his Father say. So when his dad told him to stay home, work hard, and obey—he did.

And so should you.

Why? Because we all need to grow.

And Jesus grew in wisdom and stature, and in favor with God and man.

Luke 2:52

If Jesus needed to grow, how much more do we?

Like the seed buried alone in the ground, it's in the dark seasons when no one is watching that we learn the most important lessons.[1]

2. Hidden Things Are Formed

Some of the most beautiful things in the world are formed in obscurity. Consider the development of a child in the womb.

Isolated.

Alone.

Microscopic and seemingly insignificant.

Yet God is working overtime in the secret place to create something so miraculous it brings tears to our eyes when it finally arrives.

> For you created my inmost being;
>> you knit me together in my mother's womb.
> I praise you because I am fearfully and wonderfully made;
>> your works are wonderful,
>> I know that full well.
> My frame was not hidden from you
>> when I was made in the secret place,
>> when I was woven together in the depths of the earth.
> Your eyes saw my unformed body;
>> all the days ordained for me were written in your book
>> before one of them came to be.
>
> Psalm 139:13–16

You're not forgotten, you're in formation.

As an employer must process an employee before releasing him into the workforce, our formation is necessary for God to use us.

3. Hidden Things Go Deep

Roots grow best in darkness, below the surface, under the radar.

A tree is never concerned with the height or width of its reach, but with the depth of its roots. The deeper the tree is rooted, the greater its reach will be.

The same is true for you.

Yet we can't go deeper in God if we're too busy comparing ourselves to others. May we stop looking left and right and start looking up and in. The truth is, we don't need to grow taller or wider, but deeper in him.

Yokes and Cloaks

As time passed, I believed Jesus was with me. Many mornings, I'd picture him at my kitchen table, drinking a cup of coffee. I sensed his presence as I spent years behind closed doors simply loving on my kids. God was doing a deep work in my heart. I had very little time to pray, but I sensed an intimacy with Jesus I can't explain. Somehow the isolation provided tunnel vision. With no other distractions and nothing to prove, I found myself falling head over heels in love again. When Jesus is all you have, you realize he's all you need.

You're not forgotten, you're in formation.

Jesus understands our hidden years. He experienced a hidden season no one can ever top. His own Father hid his face while he suffered on the cross. Jesus cried out, "Dad, why have you abandoned me?"

Jesus bore the weight of our sin and exchanged our cloaks of shame for his robe of righteousness. The Father turned his back on Jesus so he would never have to leave our side. Jesus wraps himself around us and we are hidden in him.

> Since, then, you have been raised with Christ, set your hearts on things above, where Christ is, seated at the right hand of God. Set your minds on things above, not on earthly things. For you died, and your life is now hidden with Christ.
>
> Colossians 3:1–3

Imagine an old wooden yoke draped over the necks of a pair of oxen heading out to plow a field. On one side is a strong ox and on the other, a puny little calf. Naturally, the seasoned ox should lead the way and train the new recruit. But the stubborn calf attempts to take control, veering in a completely different direction.

Our yoke will never feel light if we try to bear the burden by ourselves. Hiddenness feels heavy because we believe the lie that we are doing life alone. We must shift the weight toward Jesus and allow him to lead the way. Then our yoke will be easy, and our burden will feel light. To be hidden in Christ means our inward selves are at rest. We may be running around on the outside—caring for our family—but on the inside we are at peace, knowing God has our kids in the palm of his hand.

> When Jesus is all you have, you realize he's all you need.

You're not called to be everything to everyone.

Shift the weight toward Jesus.

Treading Water

"Where're we going?" Emma begged as we hiked down a dirt trail.

"It's a surprise," I said with a wink.

The path split and as we veered to the left, the sound of rushing water roared in the distance.

"What is that?" Isaac asked.

We rounded the bend and came face-to-face with a 350-foot-wide waterfall. We walked up to a slow-moving part of the river, and my oldest son, Jeremiah, asked to cross the river by hopping from one rock to the next. I nodded my head, wanting to encourage his spontaneity. Thirty seconds later, he slipped and slid straight into the river.

"I'm ruining my new Converse," Jer complained as I rolled my eyes.

At some point during the commotion, my five-year-old son, Isaac, decided to jump in. The only problem? Isaac couldn't swim. Latching onto Jeremiah, Isaac pushed him under to keep his own head above the water. This is known as instinctive drowning response, and it occurs when the person drowning panics and is no longer acting in a conscious manner. Many times, the one attempting to save the victim will die and the person drowning will live.

Frantic, I jumped in and attempted to tear my sons apart.

"Swim away!" I screamed over the roar of the falls.

Jeremiah reluctantly swam to the shore.

Meanwhile, Isaac wrapped his arms and legs around me and began pushing *me* under.

"Stop it! What are you doing?"

As I wrestled my son, I caught a glimpse of someone else in the river: my four-year-old daughter, Emma. I now had two children drowning.

I clutched my daughter under my right arm and my son under my left. I kicked my legs as fast as humanly possible as my oldest watched this horrid scene from the shore. Exhaustion kicked in, and everything in me wanted to let go and give up. I realized at that moment I couldn't save them both. I needed the strength of my arms *and* legs to carry one safely to shore. So I made a split-second decision. I released Emma and turned my back on her. I scooped Isaac up and swam away and set him on a rock. When I was confident he was okay, I knew it was time to do the one thing I was dreading.

I can't turn around. I just left my baby girl to drown. What have I done?

I whipped my head, expecting her to be gone. Yet there she was, doggie-paddling with her little nose barely above the surface.

For the next three nights, I couldn't sleep. Whenever I would drift off, I startled awake, reliving the nightmare. I ran different scenarios through my head. What if I had tried to save Emma first? Would Isaac have drowned?

On the third night, I cried out to God:

Help me. I'm tormented by this. No parent should ever have to choose to save one of their kids and leave the other one to die.

And out of the darkness of my bedroom, I heard the voice of Father God say, "You're right. I know the feeling."

PRAY THIS: *Dear Jesus, I need to know you're here with me in this hidden season. I feel alone and forgotten. I know you will never leave me in my head, but help this truth to travel to my heart. I pray this week that you show me a personal revelation of your love. Use something in my daily life to communicate to me in an intimate way that you are El Roi, the God who sees, and you see me.*

DO THIS: Grab a notebook and write down a list of one hundred things God has blessed you with. That may seem like a lot, but as you start to focus on the goodness of God, he will begin to reveal all the blessings you have overlooked. Sometimes in our hidden seasons, we hyper-focus on what we are missing out on and neglect all God has blessed us with. You are seen. You are loved. You are blessed. And remember, all hidden seasons have one thing in common—they end.

TO THE MOM TRYING TO EARN GOD'S LOVE:

Drop the song and dance. Your performance doesn't impress God. Your obedience does.

10

The Push to Perform

Jesus, shift the spotlight

The line separating good and evil passes not through states, nor between classes, nor between political parties either—but right through every human heart.

—Aleksandr Solzhenitsyn, *The Gulag Archipelago*

When I was eight, my family moved across town, and in the scurry of packing boxes and loading furniture, I fell asleep on the floor of our basement. I startled awake at the slam of the front door and rubbed the indents of the carpet off my cheek.

"Mom? Daaaaaaad?" I called out while wandering around the empty house, my voice bouncing off the bare walls like a ping-pong ball. I glanced out the picture window and realized neither of their vehicles was in the driveway.

They moved without me.

It was like the movie *Home Alone*, except there were no robbers and it wasn't funny. I threw on my coat and trudged through the snow to a gas station and begged the attendant for a quarter to use the pay phone. Dialing the only number I knew, I called my grandparents. In my parents' defense, my dad assumed I was riding with my mom, and my mom thought I was riding with my dad. But a lie took root after this episode: *I am forgettable.*

> **We tend to confuse our desire to be USED by God with our desire to be SEEN by the world.**

This false narrative morphed into the need to prove myself. Not just to my parents, but to the world. As a kid, it looked like my inability to turn down a dare. But as an adult, it translated into this line of thought:

They don't think I can do such-and-such. I'll prove them wrong.

Every one of us is a mixed bag of motives.

We tend to confuse our desire to be *used* by God with our desire to be *seen* by the world. And let me tell you, they are two very different things.

A Dare I Couldn't Resist

It all started with a stupid reality TV show.

"You could never do that, Mom," my eight-year-old son, Jeremiah, teased as we watched a woman scale an inverted climbing wall over a pool of water. We made a habit of spending time together watching reality TV, and our newest obsession was *American Ninja Warrior*.

"Yes I could," I said as I threw a handful of popcorn in my mouth.

My son and husband laughed out loud.

I went to bed with their laughter ringing in my ears. It was a harmless comment, but their words were poking at an insecurity I refused to bring to God—my deep need to prove my worth.

After all those years of hiding in my home caring for babies, I was ready to prove to the world I had something to offer. The next morning, I filled out the online application for season eight of *American Ninja Warrior*.

Mind you, I couldn't do a single pull-up, but that was a minor detail.

I started a home workout routine, and I traveled to a ninja gym three hours away. I justified the time and energy I spent training by promising God if I conquered Mount Midoriyama, I'd encourage families to adopt.

In hindsight, I imagine God was on his throne shaking his head.

Six months into my training, I asked a friend to compile a bunch of video clips of me attempting to scale rock walls and hang from apparatuses with ridiculous names like wing nuts, cliffhangers, and pipe sliders. Don't be impressed. Although my upper body strength increased, I lacked the coordination to master *any* of these obstacles. So when she created my audition video, I suggested she cut all the clips right before I fell.

On film, I looked like a ninja.

In reality, I was a puny mom of five still trying to prove herself.

Don't we do this in life? Maybe you've never gone to the extremes I have, but a part of us feels the need to prove our worth. It's the Instagram post of the Joanna Gaines living room so the world believes we are an expert interior designer. It's the photoshopped image we share on our fortieth birthday to prove we haven't aged in decades. It's the know-it-all advice we give to new moms to appear like experts in the parenting department. It's the designer purse we carry around, silently bragging to the world how well off we must be.

> If we spend all our time impressing people, we won't have time to love them.

Little did I know, God was about to whack me over the head and teach me a hard truth: if we spend all our time impressing people, we won't have time to love them.

Shifting the Spotlight

Remember how stretching our faith is like Jesus asking us to hop into a wheelbarrow as he tightrope walks across Niagara Falls? He's the one putting on the show. We tend to get it wrong. We think *we* are the ones performing. We are the ones the audience is cheering for. We are the ones who must accomplish something great for God. Pride says, "Look at me." While faith says, "Look at Jesus. Don't mind me, I'm just tagging along for the ride."

The push to perform is a temptation we're all familiar with. Whether it manifests in covering our walls with degrees or secretly hoping our children's success will validate our own, we all experience the tug to prove ourselves. It's easy to confuse the roar of the crowd for the applause of heaven.

When John baptized Jesus in the Jordan River, something amazing happened. The power of the Holy Spirit rested on Jesus and God's voice declared from the clouds, "This is my dearly loved Son, who brings me great joy."[1]

The first official mic drop

Take a second and let that sink in. God approved of Jesus before he ever performed a single miracle or did anything for him. The same is true for us. What we do for God doesn't validate his love for us. After this momentous occasion, a laser light show should have followed. Or at least, Jesus could have kicked off his ministry with a fireworks display and a massive party. Instead, the Holy Spirit grabbed Jesus by the hand and led him to the last place any of us want to go.

> Then Jesus was led by the Spirit into the wilderness to be tempted by the devil.
>
> Matthew 4:1

Stop and reread that.

The *devil* didn't escort Jesus into the wilderness, the *Holy Spirit* did. And the goal? For Jesus to be tempted.

If we desire to be like Jesus, we should expect the Holy Spirit to slip his arm around our waist and steer us toward a dry season. Why? To test our character. Your calling may propel you forward, but your lack of character will slam on the brakes. The problem lies in the fact that we tend to believe the best about ourselves and the worst about everyone else. We make statements like, "If only people knew my heart." But the truth is, *we* don't even know our hearts. The Bible says that the human heart is the most deceitful of all things. Who can know how bad it is?

> Your calling may propel you forward, but your lack of character will slam on the brakes.

Trials don't bring out the best in you or the worst in you—they uncover the *real* you.

When my kids were toddlers, we bought a solid oak toy box made by the Amish. One morning, I noticed a terrible odor in our house that I couldn't track down. I looked high and low. I cleaned our sink drain and took the garbage out. Still, the smell persisted. Several days later, my son climbed into the toy box and emptied its contents onto the living room floor. The top of his head peeked out of the box as he gnawed on something green. It was a moldy cheese stick that had been rotting for months.

We can't ask God to change us until he exposes what's festering inside. And we don't realize we need a savior until we recognize it's from our own hard hearts we need to be rescued.

Pride Comes before a Fall

I was folding laundry one night when my cell buzzed. I pulled it out of my back pocket, noticed it was a California area code, and didn't answer.

Probably a telemarketer.

But when I listened to my voicemail, I realized it was a representative from *American Ninja Warrior*. The man on the line informed me I was chosen to compete in the qualifiers in Pennsylvania. I dropped the sock whose match I was hunting for and hung up the phone in a daze.

I'm going to be on American Ninja Warrior.

Ten of my family and friends traveled with me to Philadelphia a month later. As I walked onto the set, the magnitude of my decision blinded me as much as the stage lighting.

What have I done?

After a list of rules, a lengthy check-in procedure, and some photos, the competitors were assigned numbers. I was lucky number seven. Only one woman would run the course before me. Standing on the starting platform with the clamoring crowd beside me and ten cameramen staring at me, I knew there was no turning back. Matt Iseman announced my name as I glared straight ahead at my first obstacle, the quintuple steps.

I'm going to pee my pants.

The buzzer sounded. I bounded toward the first step and held on like a cat clawing a sofa. The surface of the obstacle was rough like sandpaper to ensure contestants didn't slip. I scraped my knee on my first jump, and blood trickled down my calf. I turned my head toward the next step and vaulted in its direction. Immediately, I lost my grip and slipped off into the pool below.

When my head broke the surface of the water, a part of me was mortified. The other part of me laughed out loud.

It's just a stupid game show.

An assistant grabbed my hand and yanked me out of the water as the cameramen continued to track my every move. I walked toward the crowd to greet my husband and my son Jeremiah, who was sobbing.

"Mom, I can't believe you fell on the first obstacle," he said between sniffles.

"Why are you crying, buddy? It's *just* a game."

A few contestants later, still sopping wet and wrapped in my POM Wonderful towel, I watched an eighty-year-old Vietnam vet conquer the quintuple steps. My husband bumped my arm and said, "Look! Even that old guy made it farther than you."

The ride back to New York was a quiet one. I rested my feet on the dashboard and pulled my knees up to my chest as I gazed out the window. The thought of returning home made me more nervous than performing on national television. As much as I could brush off my fall, I felt I had failed all those who were rooting for me. I wasn't sure how I was going to break the news. And what was worse, I wouldn't know if my run would air on television until the episode launched three months later. NBC interviewed me, and I had the opportunity to share about God and our foster care journey. So I desired for this piece to be shown to the world. But if they aired my interview, they would also be airing my fall. As a mom of five, I was nicknamed The Diaper Ninja. I knew if they showcased my run, some stupid joke about my diaper getting wet would follow.

My run never made the cut. (God graciously spared me of ridicule.) But through this experience, I learned the truth of the adage "A mistake that makes you humble is better than an achievement that makes you arrogant."[2]

The Real You

When the Spirit led Jesus into the desert, he went without food or water for forty days. I'm sure he was hangry. So the enemy's first temptation was to prey upon Jesus' hunger. The devil double-dog dared him to turn a stone into bread. Jesus rebuked the enemy, throwing Scripture in his face:

> Man shall not live on bread alone, but on every word that comes from the mouth of God.[3]

The enemy loves to entice us to use our gifts for ourselves. With his second temptation, the devil upped the ante:

Then the devil took him to the holy city and had him stand on the highest point of the temple. "If you are the Son of God," he said, "throw yourself down. For it is written: 'He will command his angels concerning you, and they will lift you up in their hands.'"

Matthew 4:5–6

If I was in Jesus' shoes, no angels would be necessary. I'd backflip off the ledge, soar through the air while performing a triple axel, and land gracefully with a tuck and roll. After a victory dance, I'd dash back up the temple like it was the warped wall and hit the big red buzzer while rubbing it in the enemy's face. But this is exactly what the devil wants us to do—to waste our lives impressing others. The angels were at Jesus' disposal, the power of the Spirit coursed through his veins, and I'm sure he had the upper body strength to put on a show. Yet he refused. Rather, he reminded the devil we should not test God.

God is the one testing us.

But why? To expose our pride.

Pride goes before destruction, a haughty spirit before a fall.

Proverbs 16:18

The Bible warns us about pride. Pride isn't just a sin. It's the root of *all* sin. Every evil thing we think or do springs forth from a place of pride. Love, on the other hand, is the root of all godly living. This is why Paul taught the church in Corinth their lives were a noisy Led Zeppelin drum solo unless every good work they performed was birthed from a place of love.[4] God leads us into situations that expose the root of pride that lingers below the surface. If left unattended, this root will produce bad fruit.

When Jesus goes digging in our closets, he doesn't just pull out God dreams. Sometimes he's cleaning house, pulling out the junk in our hearts that needs to be thrown in the trash.

One of the best ways to pinpoint the pride in our lives is to answer this question: If God stripped away everything people knew you for, what would be left? Your exposed, vulnerable self. But this is who God wants to use, the *real* you. He can't do anything with the *pretentious* you.

That gal just gets in the way.

Interrogated by God

I walked into the sterile office with my head held high and my résumé in hand. The room was empty except for two metal chairs and a folding table, which glowed under the pendant light hanging above. The location resembled an interrogation scene from *Criminal Minds*. But rather than a detective, God sat across from me with his arms crossed.

I pulled out my paperwork, trying to hide my trembling hands. One by one, I spread out my accomplishments on the table. I displayed the evidence: my awards, my degrees, my talents, and my giftings. I found myself talking way too much while God remained silent. He didn't appear impressed, and I got the sense I was not nailing this interview. When I was done rambling, I took a deep breath and waited for his reply.

The side of his mouth curled upward and formed a half smile. He stood up, flipped the table, and all my important papers blew across the room. I jolted out of my seat and scurried around the room to grab them while God motioned for me to stop.

"I don't need any of this, Jess. I want *you*."

"But without it, I have nothing to offer," I said.

"Exactly. I can only fill empty things."

No Experience Necessary

If Jesus posted a help-wanted ad, it would read like this:

Help Wanted: Immediate openings. Our company is in search of an unqualified person to join our rapidly growing team. No experience necessary. No degrees required. Must be teachable, humble, and not afraid to fail. Availability trumps capability every time.

How did we get it in our heads that we need to be talented to be used by God? Most of the time, our talents get in the way. Our giftings are like toenails. They are meant to go out, not in. When we use our talents to glorify ourselves, they become giant distractions, robbing God of the attention he deserves. But when we use them to glorify God and love the world around us, those rocks in our pockets can take down giants.

Maybe when you look in the mirror you think, *I have nothing to offer.* You don't have a beautiful singing voice, so you would never join the worship team. You aren't a biblical scholar, so you can't host a Bible study. You're petrified to stand in front of a crowd, so you could never preach or teach. And let's be honest—kids' ministry is a hard pass when your whole life feels like a 24/7 vacation Bible school on steroids.

> We overestimate how God will use our talents, and we underestimate how God will use our obedience.

Can I let you in on a secret? God can *use* your talents, but he doesn't *need* your talents. He can also use a stick in the hand of a stuttering man, a stone in the sling of a scrawny boy, and the stinky mouth of a stubborn donkey. We overestimate how God will use our talents, and we underestimate how God will use our obedience.

Our giftings and abilities rarely open doors. Rather it's our failures, our weaknesses, and our surrender that turn the key and pop the pin to reveal our destinies.

PRAY THIS: *Dear Jesus, I'm afraid to pray this prayer, but I know it's necessary. Expose the pride in my heart. Forgive me for the times I've been a mixed bag of motives. I want my life to glorify you, but sometimes my pride gets in the way. Forgive me for all the times I've used the talents and abilities you gave me to shift the spotlight toward myself instead of toward you. It's not about me. It's not even about what others think of me. It's all about you.*

DO THIS: List all the roles you play in life in the larger circle below, such as wife, mother, sister, friend. Then list any jobs or titles you may have in the circle. Finally, list what you're known for: your hobbies, talents, giftings, abilities. If God stripped away everything people knew you for, what would be left is the real you. This is who God loves and who he wants to use.

TO THE DISILLUSIONED MOM:

When life feels like a giant letdown and faith a mean trick, claw your way out of the trenches and climb over your offense. I promise we will win this war.

11

The Offense of Unanswered Prayer

Jesus, train me to climb over my offense

You can't get the peace that passes understanding until you give up your right to understand.

—Bill Johnson, *Manifesto for a Normal Christian Life*

Several years ago, I was an assistant coach for a kindergarten basketball team.

Every Saturday morning, kids flooded the gym hyped up on adrenaline and Timbits. Our goal was to reinforce the basics: dribbling, shooting, and passing. But at the last practice of the season, we introduced a new game. Each child was to dribble their ball within the circle of center court. The goal was to knock the ball out of your opponent's hand. The last man standing would be declared the winner.

When the game commenced, the most experienced player, Ben, swatted the ball repeatedly from the others, causing it to roll across the court.

"You're out, Zoey," I mumbled with the whistle between my lips.

Zoey froze and glared up at me. Alligator tears welled in her eyes.

"Ben is mean. He hit the ball right out of my hand," she said.

"Honey, he's supposed to. That's the point. It's called stealing."

I realized at that moment that the kids didn't know what it felt like to have their ball stolen. It was a shock to their systems. We'd spent the whole season working on their ball-handling skills. They had never played a real game.

"Why would you let him do that?" Zoey stammered between sobs while waving her tiny finger at me.

I was being reprimanded by a five-year-old.

She stormed off the court and into her mother's arms, vowing to never play basketball again.

Many of us storm off the court of life in this same fashion.

The thief comes only to steal and kill and destroy; I [Jesus] have come that they may have life, and have it to the full.

John 10:10

Something of great value was stolen from you:

A child.

A marriage.

A dream.

Your health.

It's not supposed to be this way.

I'm right there with you. When my daughter Mara was diagnosed with severe autism, it took a full year for me to catch my breath. And then another three years before I sensed a glimmer of hope when I looked toward the future. During this time, we decided to trust God and have another baby. My greatest fear, the fear I dared not speak out loud as if to give it power: What if my son was autistic too?

Yet there I sat as the psychologist recited the results of the evaluation like a computer spitting out data—all facts, no compassion.

Keep it together, Jess.

I knew if I caught my husband's eye and sensed he was on the verge of tears, the dam would break, and I'd find myself in the middle of another panic attack.

Why would God allow this to happen—not once—but twice? The One with the whistle in his mouth, the Big Man who calls the shots, stood by and did nothing. How could a loving God not intervene? Like Zoey, staring up at me in shock, our hearts well with anger and we refuse to play on his team. If we can't trust the Coach— we're out.

> We become victims of the one who robbed us rather than victors of the One who saved us.

A spirit of passivity overtakes us.

We lose heart.

And if we lose heart, we lose everything.

Why?

Because it skews our perspective.

We become victims of the one who robbed us rather than victors of the One who saved us. And the devil loves it when we start blaming God for his handiwork.

We've Been around This Mountain Before

"Your son Jacob has Level 3 Autism."

The psychologist's voice trailed off in the distance. That was the only sentence I heard. Every other comment after this statement sounded like the teacher from Charlie Brown. We anticipated Jake was on the spectrum, but I secretly hoped it was a mild case. Jake was always happy. He was always smiling and loved to climb into everyone's lap—even strangers—which made for some awkward moments. He never experienced meltdowns or violent behavior. Yet the severity of his diagnosis was due to his lack of social skills. He had very few words, and he lived in his own little world, even to a greater degree than my daughter Mara.

We'd been around this mountain before, and I couldn't imagine my soul enduring this cyclic journey.

I was angry at God—again.

The autism diagnosis itself didn't make me angry.

I don't get it, God. We stepped out in faith. We refused to let fear dictate our decision to have a big family. We trusted you despite the odds being stacked against us. Isn't this where you're supposed to show up in glory?

No reply.

My husband explains God's silence best. He compares his relationship with God to having a best friend who shares all his secrets. This friend offers advice when we seek direction, and he imparts vision for our future and the ministry we lead. But when it comes to the question of our kids' limitations—God plays the silent game.

I pray you never know the sting of the silent treatment, but I'm certain at some point you will. The problem isn't the silence. The real issue is when we translate God's silence as proof he doesn't care. At the moment of Jake's diagnosis, I felt like the eight-year-old girl sleeping on the basement floor, forgotten by her family, invisible to her Father.

Where are you, Dad?

Why would you leave me?

When Faith Feels Like a Mean Trick

I wish I could tell you after my son's diagnosis I continued to trust God, but that would be a lie. I hid from everyone. I stopped going to church. I blamed my absence on my circumstances, but family and friends offered numerous times to watch my kids on

Sundays. I couldn't face God or people. I didn't even tell my closest friends about the diagnosis, and when they found out, I refused to talk about it. I kept picturing God as the mean kid, Sid, from *Toy Story*, and I was his pet hermit crab. Faith felt like a cruel trick as God poked me with a stick and I retreated farther and farther into my shell.

Eventually, Jake enrolled in the same ABA program as Mara, and at three years old, he climbed onto a bus to start intensive one-on-one therapy. His time away from home was a reprieve, but the empty house left me with my thoughts, and my thoughts took me by the hand and dragged me into a downward spiral.

Do you know what's worse than hitting rock bottom?

When you discover it's *not* rock bottom. Rather, all this time you've been sitting on top of a trap door, and when that door gives way, you fall farther than you ever thought possible.

The Great Fall

I went through the motions of caring for my kids, but I felt numb. A callus is formed after a repeated injury, causing the skin to thicken as a way of protecting itself from future pain.

This was my heart.

To make matters worse, my adopted daughter, Emma, was giving us a run for our money. When she started school, daily calls from her teacher sounded like this:

"Good morning, Mrs. Hurlbut. Emma is having a rough day."

"Again? What happened?" I asked.

"Well, she threw a chair at her friends when she wasn't chosen as line leader."

Apparently, in Head Start, they don't just teach letters and numbers, they also teach you how to swear like a sailor. One of her classmates possessed quite the vocabulary, and Emma loved to repeat anything that would gain her negative attention. So sometimes the phone calls included chair-throwing *and* curse words.

Several months into her schooling, Emma developed a fever that wouldn't go away. This only caused her behaviors to escalate. After eleven days of sickness, I called our pediatrician. The visit started out like any other until the doctor took her temperature.

"How long has she had a fever?"

"Eleven days," I said.

The smile on the pediatrician's face flattened as she listened to Emma's breathing.

"What's wrong?" I asked.

"We need to walk Emma over to the emergency room to run some tests."

We followed the speed-walking doctor across the parking lot to the hospital. They pricked her, prodded her, and wheeled her in for scans and X-rays; all the while Emma begged to go home.

"Your daughter has a mass on her lung the size of a grapefruit," the ER doctor announced, emotionless. My mind failed to compute his words. The day felt like a whirlwind. One minute we were at the pediatrician's office, and the next minute we were whisked away on a MedFlight to Boston Children's Hospital.

The following morning, a team of doctors paraded into our room dressed in hazmat suits to report their latest findings. It was as if they were speaking a foreign language and I only caught the scary words: oncology, tumor, cancer, and infectious disease. At one point, her lung collapsed.

That night, I climbed over the side rail of the hospital bed and curled up to my baby girl, maneuvering my way around the tubes and wires. My arm rose and fell in sync with her labored breathing. Just when I thought she was asleep, she rolled over—her eyes welling with emotion.

"I want to go home, Mommy. Please, let me go home," she begged while squeezing my fingers as hard as she could.

"Not yet, honey. The doctors have to figure out what's wrong," I reminded her as I choked back the tears.

While she slept, I refused to let her go. I was terrified she wouldn't make it through the night. A million worst-case scenarios ran through my mind. I envisioned myself banging on a locked door in heaven plastered with deadbolts.

In my darkest hour, I pleaded with God:

Father, take this away. I will do anything. Let me switch places with her.

Why her? Why not me?

I repeated this prayer for hours until I drifted off to sleep.

Reprimanding God

The next morning, a team of twelve doctors returned to our airtight hospital room. Suited from head to toe in PPE, they explained that Emma may have an infectious disease. This required her and me to remain in isolation until they ruled out some possibilities.

I thought I was a shut-in before, but this took things to a whole new level. As soon as the doctors left the room, I made my getaway to the only place I could—the adjacent bathroom. I stood in the shower for thirty minutes, hoping to wake up from this nightmare. As the steam filled the room and the hot water beat against my face, mixing with my tears, I reprimanded God, waving my little finger at him.

This costs too much, God. I didn't sign up for this. My kids are a casualty of war.

I wasn't sure who to blame—myself for being stupid enough to jump onto the court in faith or the Man with the whistle in his mouth who stood by and did nothing.

The Counterattack

Our anger is valid, but what if it's pointed at the wrong person?

Listen to me, the ball was stolen from you because you are a great threat, and the strategy of the opposing team is to take out the best players first.

Finally, be strong in the Lord and in his mighty power. Put on the full armor of God, so that you can take your *stand* against the devil's schemes. For our struggle is not against flesh and blood, but against the rulers, against the authorities, against the powers of this dark world and against the spiritual forces of evil in the heavenly realms. Therefore put on the full armor of God, so that when the day of evil comes, you may be able to *stand* your ground, and after you have done everything, to *stand*.

Ephesians 6:10–13, italics added

We're not in Kansas anymore.

If God instructs us to strap on armor—this means war. You may be completely unaware of it, but there is a spiritual battle raging right above your head. And sometimes, we suffer casualties. The Bible warns us that the devil plans, schemes, and strategizes to take us out. His primary goal is to steal, kill, and destroy. And one of the enemy's best tactics is to convince you *God* is the one stealing, killing, and destroying. Because if he can entice you to make God your target, he's drafted you onto his team. One devastating blow and suddenly you're fighting a battle *against* God rather than *for* him.

I don't care how beat down you feel or how much you want to bail. God promises to never leave us alone. He is on the battlefield with us. And this is the part I love: God doesn't ask us to *fight back* but to *stand up*. Jesus fought for us two thousand years ago and won. And from this place of victory, he will supply all the strength we need to stand. If we ask the Holy Spirit to empower us, he can give us the strength to claw our way out of the trenches.

The Point of No Return

Later that night, I sat in the dark with my eyes glued to Emma's monitor, praying for her oxygen levels to increase. Greg reached across the hospital bed and grabbed my hand, rubbing my palm in a circular motion with his thumb.

"It's just too much—all of this," I whispered, trying not to wake Emma.

"I know," Greg said, shaking his head.

"I'm so mad at God. I want to walk away, but where else would we go?"

"It's like we know too much to go back, but it costs too much to move forward," Greg admitted.

Greg's words hung like a thick fog in the dark hospital room. We spent the next hour sitting in silence with the rhythm of the heart monitor beeping in our ears. I imagined us back in college, trying to scale the stucco wall we had jumped off in faith. With our knees scraped up and our hearts heavy, we realized there was no going back. Our journey of faith was shoving us forward whether we liked it or not.

Forty Days and Forty Nights

We spent forty days and nights at Boston Children's Hospital. Because we did not have family close by, we had to find childcare for our kids back home. Saying our situation out loud sounded insane:

"We are currently isolated by the infectious disease department at Boston Children's Hospital. Our youngest daughter has a mass the size of a grapefruit on her lung, which is a medical anomaly. In the meantime, we have to secure twenty-four-hour care for our four other children, two of whom struggle with severe autism."

Have you ever been offended by your life?

I sure have.

I'm sure our situations differ, but the frustration is the same. How do we move forward when we're banging on the door of heaven and it feels as if it's dead-bolted shut? How do we trust God when our desperate prayers for our kids seemingly go unanswered?

At one point in Jesus' ministry, John the Baptist was in prison awaiting death row. He heard rumors of healings and miracles. Yet he lay in a rodent-infested prison wondering if he'd ever set eyes on a sunrise again. Why would Jesus deliver and rescue so many others, but neglect his own cousin? So John sends a message to Jesus by way of one of his disciples:

Are you the one who is to come, or shall we look for another?

Matthew 11:3 ESV

John baptized Jesus himself and witnessed God's voice proclaiming from heaven that Jesus was his beloved son. Why would he ever question if Jesus was the Messiah? Because when all we see are locked doors and concrete walls, it's easy to doubt in our hearts what we know to be true in our heads.

John was offended by his life.

And maybe you are too.

But what was Jesus' response?

Go and tell John what you hear and see: the blind receive their sight and the lame walk, lepers are cleansed and the deaf hear, and the dead are raised up, and the poor have good news preached to them. And *blessed is the one who is not offended by me.*

Matthew 11:4–6 ESV, italics added

Our greatest blessings are on the other side of our offense.

I was waiting on God to remove my problems. But it's not God's job to remove the offense, it's my job to climb over it. In another translation, Jesus says it this way: "Blessed is anyone who does not stumble on account of me."[1] We only stumble over things we refuse to step over. The ball is in our court. Jesus longed for John and for us to realize this truth: Just because God is not meeting *your* expectations, doesn't mean he's not fulfilling *his* promises. It's natural to be offended in the moment, but harboring offense in our hearts is a conscious choice, and this is where the devil trips us up. The offense of unanswered prayer—if left to grow—cultivates a spirit of envy. "Envy is when you resent God's goodness in other people's lives and ignore God's goodness in your own."[2] We must climb over our offense and run after Jesus. Our biggest breakthroughs are found on the other side of our offense.

Your Unanswered Prayers

What stumbling block is between you and God? What prayer has God failed to answer that you can't see past? Jesus has more for your life. He wants to use you in amazing ways, and the enemy knows it. His goal is to do whatever it takes to convince you to storm off the court and sit on the bench. He's threatened by your presence and desires to draft you onto his team. We must be aware of his schemes and strategies.

World War I was a war fought in the trenches. Both sides dug channels as a defensive military tactic. These trenches provided protection from the enemy's fire. But early mornings were the prime time for a surprise attack. Because of this, each day, an hour before dawn, soldiers were given the stand-to order. All men on the front line were commanded to stand on the fire step with their rifles in hand, watching for the enemy's advancement.

In our darkest hour, God calls us to climb out of the trenches and stand at attention—chin up, chest out, shoulders back, stomach in. He provides the full armor of God for our protection.[3] The helmet of salvation reminds us Jesus is the One who *saves* us, not the one who *attacks* us. The belt of truth, worn close to the body, symbolizes our need to cling to God's truth and allow it to surround us. The shield of faith deflects the arrows of doubt the enemy hurls. The sword of the Spirit proclaims the unshakable Word of God over our wavering emotions of unbelief. The breastplate of righteousness guards our hearts against the lie that roars, "You're not good enough."

God's not searching for professional fighters. He's looking for good standers.

When God looks down from heaven, he doesn't see an insecure woman on the battlefield—he sees his Son. Jesus wraps himself around you and me, concealing our imperfections and hiding us in his perfect love.

God's not searching for professional fighters. He's looking for good standers. We must claw our way out of the trenches, dust the gravel off our knees, and stand in the victory Jesus paid for us on the cross. It's always darkest before dawn. I promise you, we win this war.

PRAY THIS: *Dear Jesus, forgive me for believing the lie that you are against me rather than for me. Forgive me for accusing you of apathy when it comes to my struggles. Help me to realize I'm a threat to the enemy and all the loss I have experienced is his handiwork, not yours. Sometimes I want to retreat, but I choose to climb out of the trenches and stand to my feet. I proclaim your truth and Word over my life as I stand in your victory.*

DO THIS: The only offensive weapon God has given us is the sword of his Spirit. We don't fight with our hands but with our mouths. Proclaim the fifteen identity statements below out loud. Why? Because the enemy can't read your mind; only God can. If we are to fight against his lies, we need to speak God's truth out loud with authority. (Feel free to come back to this list anytime the enemy is hurling doubt or unbelief at you. This is how we fight our battles.)

1. I am a child of God. (John 1:12)
2. I am a saint. (1 Corinthians 1:2 ESV)
3. I am protected by the power of his name. (John 17:11)
4. I have peace with God. (Romans 5:1)
5. I have been justified by faith. (Romans 5:1)
6. I am free from the cycle of sin and death. (Romans 8:2)

7. I am led by the Spirit of God. (Romans 8:14)

8. I am a joint heir with Christ. (Romans 8:17)

9. I am confident that all things work together for good. (Romans 8:28)

10. I am inseparable from the love of God. (Romans 8:35–39)

11. I am more than a conqueror through Christ Jesus. (Romans 8:37)

12. I have been bought with a price. (1 Corinthians 6:20)

13. I am triumphant in Christ. (2 Corinthians 2:14)

14. I am a sweet-smelling fragrance, manifesting the presence of God wherever I go. (2 Corinthians 2:14)

15. I am a new creation in Christ. (2 Corinthians 5:17)

TO THE GUILT-RIDDEN MOM:

*Every would've, should've,
could've will rob you of
the time you do have.*

12

The Guilt Trip

Jesus, take care of my kids

As believers, we aren't to be held hostage to guilt from ourselves or other people.

—Crystal McDowell, *Seriously God?*

Mom Guilt—/mäm gilt/ *noun*
- The never-ending emotion of falling short as a mother.
- The feeling that as a mom you are being selfish doing something other than caring for your family.
- The supernatural ability to disregard all things done for one's family and hyper-focus on the one thing *not* being done.

You're Fired

"I hate you, you b*tch!" My five-year-old daughter Emma screamed as the nurse prepped the needle. Headstart's lessons on swearing were paying off.

Everyone in the room, including my husband and I, picked our jaws up off the floor. After repeated blood tests and procedures at Boston Children's Hospital, we *all* wanted to scream profanities. Only my daughter didn't have a filter.

As parents, it was embarrassing.

As pastors, it was mortifying.

When I wasn't stressing about the mass in my daughter's chest, I was laden with guilt as a mom.

Where did we go wrong? We should have disciplined her more. Why is she so angry?

There is truth to the saying "Behind every great kid is a mom who is pretty sure she is screwing it up."[1]

All lies have a root. Guilt's root: *I'm not doing enough.*

Maybe if I took Emma to the doctor sooner, she wouldn't be this sick. Maybe if I paid more attention to Mara's speech, she would have been diagnosed sooner. Maybe if we hadn't wanted a big family, we wouldn't be in this mess. If motherhood were an official job, I would have fired myself years ago.

Whether you're a working mom who blames herself for the time spent away or a stay-at-home mom who feels guilty for wanting a break, we all experience the overwhelming sense that we aren't cut out for this job.

Guess what? We're not.

We all stink at parenting when we start.

But how long are we going to beat ourselves up over a past Jesus erased? Each one of us is in desperate need of God's grace.

How long are we going to beat ourselves up over a past Jesus erased?

Grace is the undeserved favor of God demonstrated by Jesus' death for all the ways we fall short. And here is the news flash: we don't have what it takes to be good parents. We need buckets of grace to bridge the chasm between our good intentions and our shortcomings.

Therefore, if anyone is in Christ, the new creation has come: The old has gone, the new is here!

2 Corinthians 5:17

Me: "God, make me better."

God: "Nah, I'd rather make you new."

In traditional Japanese art, liquid gold was used to bind together fragments of broken pottery. Each crack was etched in gold leaf and formed into a new creation—one whose brokenness and faults are completely apparent—yet stunning. Ask for God's grace to fill the cracks of your life and let him mold you into the perfectly imperfect parent he has called you to be.

Our Easter Miracle

Our church prayed for Emma daily. That's the beauty of the body of Christ. When you are at your weakest, God will rally prayer warriors around you to hold you up, just as Aaron steadied Moses's arms until God's people won the victory.[2] A week into our stay, Emma's fever broke, and two days before Easter we were released from the hospital. A month later, we found ourselves waiting on the results of her scan at a follow-up appointment.

"This doesn't make sense," the pulmonologist said, staring at the image of her CT scan while tapping his pen on the desk.

"What?" I asked.

"Tumors don't shrink. They grow or they stay the same. They don't shrink without treatment."

"But they *can* shrink with prayer," I said as I caught Greg's eye and squeezed his hand.

The doctor smirked and wheeled his chair across the room, "*Apparently.* The mass in your daughter's chest was the size of a grapefruit, and now it's the size of a lemon."

And here is the most amazing part: our church continued to pray after this good report—and the tumor *continued* to shrink. Each scan left the doctors scratching their heads, while each appointment left us doing a happy dance in the parking lot. The experts were never able to determine the cause of the mass, but to this day, her chart describes the case as a medical miracle.

I want to reignite hope in your heart. God is bigger than cancer, tumors, addictions, or neurological disorders. It doesn't matter how far your child has wandered or how long they have suffered, his desire is to heal and restore. I often wonder why God chose to heal Emma while my two kids on the spectrum continue to struggle. But as I mature in Christ, I'm learning to nestle into my Dad's arms and rest in the mystery of his will.

The Savior Complex

When my daughter Mara was first diagnosed, I spent a week at the Autism Treatment Center. I met other special-needs parents, but instead of feeling encouraged, I left feeling guilty. It seemed other moms were doing so much more to help their children than I was.

I found myself hiding away in my car, eating lunch by myself instead of socializing in the cafeteria. In the middle of my rant, God punched me in the gut with this thought:

Jess, I never called you to fix Mara, I called you to love her.

Do you realize we aren't our children's saviors?

If I've learned anything from multiple autism diagnoses and our hospital stay in Boston, it's that we can't save our kids. We can't protect them from every bully on the playground. We can't deliver them from sickness, loss, or learning disabilities. We can't rescue them from peer pressure, party scenes, or prodigal seasons. But for some unfathomable reason, we keep trying to. Because there is nothing worse than a mom who feels helpless. We would give our lives for our children, bear their heartaches, and shoulder their burdens if God allowed us.

But he doesn't.

If we spend our lives trying to save our kids, they will rely on *us* rather than their *Savior*. Jesus won't allow our codependent tendencies to block the work he wants to do in their hearts.

There is a story in the Bible about a barren woman named Hannah. For years, she pleaded with God for a baby. Her husband's second wife, Peninnah, bore him children, and she loved to rub Hannah's infertility in her face. Thankfully, none of us have second wives to compete with, but that same tormenting spirit of shame is still operating today. Mom guilt taunts us, throwing in our face all the ways we don't measure up. The name *Peninnah* comes from the Hebrew verb *pana*, which means to turn toward. Guilt's goal is to distract us from serving God. But Hannah refused to allow this mocking spirit to detour her. Rather, it drove her to the feet of the One who heard her heart's cry. Eventually, God blessed her with a son named Samuel, which means God has heard. God's ears are tuned in when we pray for our kids. He is the One who hears, and *he* is the One who saves. Don't allow mom guilt to distract you from serving Jesus.

> If we spend our lives trying to save our kids, they will rely on US rather than their SAVIOR.

But this isn't the most miraculous part of the story. Once Samuel was weaned at three years old, Hannah presented her son to Eli the priest and dedicated him to God to be raised in the temple.[3] Do you know the greatest gift a mother can give her child? To bust open the doors of heaven, boldly approach his throne, and place our kids in his loving hands. After all, our children are on loan. He's their real dad and he loves them far more than we ever could.

So, when you slip into mom-guilt mode, recognize it as a tactic of the enemy to steal your affection from Jesus. Instead of dwelling on all the ways you've fallen short, run to his feet and pray for your kids. Our prayers are the track, and his power is the train—no one is going anywhere without it.

Guilt That Holds Us Captive

Not only can mom guilt distract us, it can hold us hostage from all God has created us to be. I believe that if every mom rose up in faith and did the things God laid on her heart, the world would look dramatically different. The kingdom of heaven would advance rapidly. The enemy loves to convince us that we must make a choice: God *or* family. He wants us to believe it's an either/or decision. But with the power of the Holy Spirit, we are equipped to live a both/and life. We can care for our children *and* open up our home to a foster child. We can be a great wife *and* be a phenomenal Sunday school teacher. We can spend quality time with our families on Saturday night *and* pray for teens at youth group on Sunday night.

It's not about doing more, but rather not neglecting one role by elevating the other. God wants to use each of us in mighty ways *inside* and *outside* the home. Our circumstances don't need to change. Our season of life doesn't need to shift. Our faith needs to grow.

Five years ago, I received a heart transplant from Jesus. My new ticker beats for the kids in our country who desperately need a forever family. Once we became foster parents, I discovered there were 110,000 kids in care who were freed to be adopted—but no one wanted them. I know that is not the politically correct way to say it, but it's the truth. Most of these children have special needs, are in sibling groups, or are minorities. The families that do consider adoption long for the perfect child, leaving all those who don't fit the mold trapped in the system.

I couldn't wrap my mind around this. I knew hundreds of couples who dreamed of having a family. I had friends who spent thousands of dollars on fertility treatments. Others who flew across the world to adopt, spending more for a child than our house cost. Yet in our own backyard currently 125,000 kids go to bed each night praying for a mom and dad.

One morning, I was out for a jog on my normal route when God challenged me about the amount of time I spent running. It was a hobby I enjoyed, but I had never surrendered it to him. God was asking me to use this talent to glorify him and raise awareness for these kids in care who needed a forever family.

As I approached my neighborhood, I stopped to catch my breath. I leaned over with my hands on my knees when I felt the Holy Spirit drop a thought in my mind that has changed the course of my life:

If you take care of my kids, I'll take care of yours.

Sweaty, snot-nosed, and with tears running down my face and plopping onto the pavement, I felt the weight of this decision. *Run for them*, a still small voice echoed in my spirit.

It's counterintuitive to believe that the best thing we can do to care for our kids is to adopt more, many of whom have special needs. Yet through my journey I realized this glorious truth:

> Give, and it will be given to you. A good measure, pressed down, shaken together and running over, will be poured into your lap. For with the measure you use, it will be measured to you.
>
> Luke 6:38

This verse refers to the Jewish custom of dry measure. A generous person who was selling a sack of corn or grain would shake the basket and press the product down to fit more. The most generous vendors would even fill the sack to the point of overflowing. We can't out-give God. Yet the second sentence is the clincher for me: "with the measure *you* use, it will be measured to you."

If you take care of my kids, I'll take care of yours.

Imagine a teaspoon in my hand. With it, I scoop a measure of myself out and I offer it to God. I may be feeling extra generous, and I dip my spoon in again and offer that much of myself to others. Now visualize God, ever so politely, taking this tiny utensil from my hand. With it, he scoops up the same measure of his heavenly blessings and resources and pours them out over my life. God limits his blessings to our measurement system.

There is more to life than looking out for you and your own.

Open your heart.

Open your hands.

Open your home.

And watch God back up his dump truck and pour out a blessing that you can't contain.

Speaking My Dreams Out Loud

I tucked the kids into bed, headed back downstairs, and plunked down on the couch next to Greg, who was fiddling with his phone.

"I want to run to raise awareness for adoption," I said, biting my lip.

"That would be awesome. Where is the run?" Greg asked.

"I don't want to *join* a run—I want to *start* one. I want to try to run 110 miles to symbolize the 110,000 kids in foster care who need to be adopted."

"That's a long run. Over how many days?" Greg asked.

"Actually, I want to run the whole distance on National Adoption Day in November."

"All by yourself?" Greg said while shaking his head.

"I know it sounds irrational, but I feel like God wants me to do this."

And instead of listing off all the reasons this feat would be impossible, my amazing husband sat down at the dining room table. He started mapping out a 110-mile loop through our county, beginning in our hometown. Greg worked behind the scenes to build a website, recruit volunteers, and create a social media campaign. While I spent six months training, my husband was the engine that propelled me forward into all God planned.

You may be thinking right now, *I could never do something like that. Great things are for special people.* But we are *all* great because the power of the Holy Spirit dwells inside of us. We designed t-shirts for the run and on the back we printed my favorite quote:

> I am only one; but still I am one. I cannot do *everything*; but still I can do *something*; and because I cannot do *everything*, I will not refuse to do the *something* that I can do. [4]

This message is one God desires every mom to hear. If you feel small and insignificant, you are. But so is a stone. If you feel you have nothing to offer, you don't. But neither did a twelve-year-old shepherd boy. The stone was unremarkable. The boy, ordinary. But just as David flung one stone in faith at Goliath, our ordinary lives become extraordinary when the power of God is behind us.

What stones in your pocket need dusting off? What talents can you offer to God? What resources do you have that if placed in God's hands could be multiplied to bless the multitudes? Jesus calls us to ask for nations, while we're over here asking for him to heal a hangnail. All we can see is our limits, but God sees his Son and the untapped potential of the Holy Spirit within us.

National Adoption Day

I woke on National Adoption Day, November 16, 2018, to the first snowstorm of the year. Schools were delayed and canceled across the county. I rolled over and peered out the snow-covered window lattice at the three-inch accumulation.

"What are we going to do?" I asked my husband.

"We're gonna run," Greg said.

"*I'm* gonna run, you mean. *You're* gonna drive behind me and eat donuts," I said while rolling my eyes and shoving him over in bed.

Seriously, God? You couldn't hold back the snow until tomorrow?

A friend lent me a pair of ice cleats and met me at the door of our kids' elementary school. The whole school assembled in the cafeteria to hear me share on adoption. I displayed pictures of my family and explained that one of their classmates, my son, was adopted. I reminded them how blessed they were to grow up in good homes with a mom and dad but that there were 110,000 kids who didn't have a family.

A six-year-old girl with a high ponytail sat cross-legged on the floor, waving her hand wildly the entire time I spoke. Finally, I walked toward her, "Do you have a question, sweetie?"

"Why doesn't anyone want them?" she asked.

"I don't know, honey."

A moment of heaviness settled on the room as the kids sat in shock that 110,000 children had no parents to love them, no dinner table to eat at, and no house to call home.

"That's why I'm doing this run, so more people know these kids exist and they need a forever family."

After the assembly, I laced up my sneakers, threw on snow gear, and headed out to the parking lot to start the run with my ten-year-old son by my side.

"You ready, buddy?" I asked Jeremiah, who was going to run the first few miles with me. He looked more nervous than I was.

"I guess so," he said.

We waved goodbye and jogged down the adjacent street with the cheers of one hundred and fifty children trailing off in the distance.

This is what I was made for.

This is going to sound outlandish, but the whole world is waiting on *you* to realize who you are. The Bible says all of creation is on its tippy toes in anticipation for you to wake up and come into your own.[5] We were made for eternity, and with the power of the Holy Spirit in us, we can accomplish infinitely more than we could ever imagine. You are not just a mom, a wife, or a nobody from nowhere who has nothing to offer. You are a world changer, a city on a hill, a daughter of the Most High King. All of creation is holding its breath, longing for the day you realize this. Maybe that day is today.

The Last Mile

We broke the 110-mile run up into five-mile legs. On each leg, a pacer ran with me to keep me company and keep me moving. The first thirty miles were glorious. I was so energized by the people who stood on their porches and doorways to cheer me on. Fire departments gathered their trucks and sounded their sirens. I ran through a Native American reservation, and the entire foster care unit showed up with music, lights, and signs promoting adoption. They even provided me with a police escort. My gloves were soaked, not due to the snow but because I couldn't stop crying. It was the only tissue I could come up with. I never imagined the community would rally around me as they did. I felt like George Bailey at the end of the movie *It's a Wonderful Life* as he dashed down the snow-covered streets of Bedford Falls.

Hello, Massena! Hello, Sunoco MiniMart! Merry Christmas, you old Tackle and Bait Shop! Merry Christmas!

It wasn't Christmas but it sure felt like it. My face hurt from smiling at the kids who stood on their porches to wave, or the old farmer who stopped his tractor and shouted across his field, "I read about you in the paper!" There are very few moments in life where it feels like the world stops spinning and you know without a doubt you are doing what God created you to do.

I ran all morning. I ran all afternoon. I ran through dinner, eating my meals on the go. I ran through the night into the wee hours of early morning. At four in the morning, I was no longer running but hobbling. I never anticipated the toil my legs would take due to the metal cleats I was wearing. My feet were so swollen that I could not get my sneakers off. My husband was exhausted. To ensure I was safe, he trailed behind me in our SUV, shining the headlights to alert oncoming traffic a runner was on the road. He hadn't slept in twenty-one hours. My friend Courtney, who was a fellow foster mom, reached out and asked if she could help. Her husband offered to drive so Greg could rest in the backseat while Courtney climbed out of the car and walked with me.

As I hobbled along, wincing with each step, Courtney said nothing.

She simply grabbed my arm and interlocked it with her own. We walked silently arm-and-arm, one foot in front of the other into the darkness. The cold air burned our lungs, and we caught a glimpse of our breath as we exhaled.

Every few minutes Courtney would lean over and whisper, "You've got this. Just keep going, Jess."

Sometimes life is busting with excitement. People are on the sidelines cheering your name and rooting for you. Other times, you're exhausted and freezing, hobbling alone in the dark in the middle of nowhere. But if you listen close enough, you'll hear the Father whisper, "You've got this. Just keep going." Maybe the future scares you. When you look ahead, you don't feel like you have much faith. But you don't need faith for the future. Just faith for today. It's not a leap or a journey, it's a walk—one foot in front of the other.

The Surprise Ending

At mile sixty-eight, my husband pulled beside me in our Honda Pilot and rolled down his window.

"How's it going?"

I stared ahead, annoyed at such a stupid question.

"I figured it out. At this rate, we are ten hours behind schedule. I think you need to call it quits," Greg said.

"I can't," I responded while his calculations sank in.

"It's four a.m.; you can't keep this up. You're going to injure yourself."

With prodding from my husband and my friend Courtney, I finally caved and climbed into the car, defeated.

"Well, let's go home already," I snapped.

"We can't leave yet. You need to tell everyone you can't run any farther."

"Tell who?" I asked. "It's four a.m."

"All the people who are following you online."

Little did I know, my husband was uploading video footage onto our Facebook page and people were sharing it. He pulled out his phone and showed me videos with hundreds of comments and thousands of views.

"People are still up following me?"

I reluctantly hopped on Facebook Live and shared how I was unable to run due to the swelling in my feet and legs. I felt as if I had let the world down. But what happened next forever changed me. After we posted the video, our cell phones rang with people offering to meet us where we were and run the next leg. Over the next hour, dozens of runners contacted us and Greg coordinated who would run and when. My husband continued to trail the runners while I went home to get some rest. By ten the next morning, the last few runners were heading back toward our hometown, and we decided to meet them and walk the last quarter mile.

As we pulled up to the traffic light, we discovered a hundred people from our community gathered to walk the last quarter mile with us. I shuffled out of the car, sorer than I was the night before, and we all paraded up the highway together. We ended the run in our church parking lot, and I found myself ugly crying the entire way. I couldn't speak, so my husband stepped in.

"This is the way it was supposed to be. We can never meet this need on our own. It takes a village. Jessica can't solve this problem. We all have to do our part. So thank you for being a beautiful visual of what adoption looks like."

The crowd erupted, and slowly the narrative on foster care and adoption shifted in our community. During the following year, the number of foster homes in our county nearly doubled, and the ripple effect continues to this day.

A rock that remains alone remains small and insignificant.

But that same rock thrown in faith creates a ripple effect that lasts long after the rock is gone.

PRAY THIS: *Dear Jesus, drown out the voices that tell me I'm not doing enough as a mom. I know I fail on a daily basis, but you look past my struggles and into my heart. Help me not to elevate my role as a mom above my relationship with you. I know I can't be my children's savior. They desperately need you, and I don't want to get in the way. Teach me how to put you first in all I do. I surrender every talent and gift I have to you. I'm sorry for focusing inward. Help me to look up from my worries and look out toward a broken world.*

DO THIS: Refer back to the circle activity in chapter 10 and list all your talents, giftings, and hobbies below. Pray through each one individually and offer your talents up to God. Listen to hear if the Holy Spirit highlights one that you can use in this season of life for God's glory. Remember, giftings are like toenails. They're meant to go out, not in.

My Talents • My Abilities • My Hobbies • The Holy Spirit's Direction

The Legacy of the Long Game

Jesus, make my life count

How completely satisfying to turn from our limitations to a God who has none.

—A.W. Tozer, *The Knowledge of the Holy*

I watched a TED Talk that changed my life, and it is now a filter I run all my decisions through. The speaker, Matthew Dicks, shared how when he was twenty-two years old, the local McDonald's he managed was robbed. He found himself pressed against a greasy tile floor with a gun pinned to his head. The trigger was pulled twice, and Matt's fear morphed into regret as he realized he had done nothing with his life. For the next two decades, he suffered from Post Traumatic Stress Disorder. Despite all Matt's success, a part of him is still lying on that greasy tile floor. From this perspective, Matt offers the audience a strategy to use when we are faced with a decision. Rather than relying on the forty-year-old version of himself to make up his mind, he looks to the future and envisions himself as an old man. Matt asks the one-hundred-year-old version of himself to make the decision for him. He begs the audience to stop living in the moment but rather play the long game.[1]

Jesus is into the long, long game.

Instead of asking the one-hundred-year-old version of ourselves what to do, what if we asked our eternal selves? What if we viewed our decisions through the camera lens of eternity?

> I consider that our present sufferings are not worth comparing with the glory that will be revealed in us.
>
> Romans 8:18

Let's simplify this verse and write it as a mathematical equation:

Suffering < Glory

If you were sitting in front of me, I would be waving my arms and screaming as if you were driving the wrong way down a one-way street.

Why? Because most of my life I've been going the wrong way and so have you. I focused on forward motion rather than heavenly promotion. I'm an eighties child, so track with my old-school analogy for a second:

Imagine you're Mario from the original Super Mario Bros. Nintendo game. And if you're anything like me, I like to get places fast. So you hold down the X and Y buttons on your controller to dash through a level. While you're running toward your destination, Tetris blocks fall from the sky and halt your progress. You fly over the first few with ease, but the farther you get, the faster the blocks fall. Eventually, you throw the controller across the room in frustration. Game over. You sit frozen in the middle of the Tetris blocks as they fall around you, trapping you within their walls.

This was my life.

Things got hard, and for a season I stopped running toward God. But listen to me: Jesus is not focused on your forward motion. He doesn't measure success by how far we go, how many levels we conquer, or how many gold stars we earn. Our goals are horizontal, but God's callings are vertical. The trials in your life aren't obstacles but stepping-stones, and the limits you're frustrated by are actually your credentials.

"You're going the wrong way!"

If you were able to view your life through a camera lens and zoom out, you'd realize those Tetris blocks aren't halting your progress. They are a necessity. Each one stacks upon the other, building a staircase toward heaven. The only way you will reach the goal of looking more like Jesus is by climbing this flight of stairs. This is how God in his wisdom can use every evil thing that comes against us to work toward our good. The enemy is foolishly focused on forward motion too. He will try anything to trip us up or make us quit. But each attack only aids in our progress, as long as we keep going. Henry Ward Beecher says it best, "Troubles are often the tools by which God fashions us for better things."[2]

I *had* a dream to be used by God.

And the truth is, that dream wasn't derailed, or sidetracked, it just took an alternative route. Looking back at the forty-one years I have lived on this planet, I often tell people, "I would have never imagined my life to be this hard." But in the same breath, I say, "But I never fathomed God would use me this much." Isn't this the perfect picture of surrender? Faith is believing God has more for your life, while surrender releases the need to define *what* that more is.

And the work God calls us to do starts on the inside. It's less about *where* we're going and more about *who* we are becoming. God must do a deep work in us before he can ever birth a great work out of us.

Trust the process.

The Legacy I Want to Leave

Last week, my eight-year-old daughter busted open my bedroom door and walked in on me worshiping. The Alexa was blaring, and I was kneeling with my eyes closed and my arms raised.

"You're funny, Mom," she snickered and walked out of the room.

I was embarrassed for a minute, but then I realized I don't have a college savings account in her name. My retirement fund isn't impressive. Besides an old piano and a few mementos, I don't possess much of value to leave my children when I die. But I do have one treasure to pass on: my faith. There is a spiritual inheritance we can transfer to the next generation. When God looks down at you, he doesn't see a single person. He stands outside of time and sees generations. He is the God of Abraham, Isaac, and Jacob.

> Our kids can't BE something until they SEE something.

What if rather than focusing on our kids' behavior, their grades, their achievements, or their futures—we focused on becoming the person God created us to be? Because our kids can't *be* something until they *see* something. What if the greatest inheritance we could pass on is our passionate walk with Jesus?

So may your kids remember how you worshiped with abandon.

May they catch you praying out loud.

May they read old journals and learn you were madly in love with Jesus.

May they see you give until it hurts and forgive when it doesn't make sense.

May they stand in awe as you climb over offense and push through the pain.

May your home be filled with praise and your table filled with people.

You may not have much to give—but give your all to Jesus.

Because our faith is the greatest legacy we could ever leave.

Acknowledgments

Greg: Thank you to the man who held my hand when we received each heartbreaking diagnosis, who shoveled the sidewalks and drove twenty-four hours during my adoption run, who bought me lunch in high school when I was too poor to afford it, who followed me all the way to college in Florida, who cried the day I confessed I couldn't trust anyone, who sold the only truck he ever owned to provide for his family, who was brave enough to say yes to my wild dreams of adoption twice, and who never gave up on God no matter how difficult things got. Your faith astounds me. Your love for the church floors me. This book and this life wouldn't exist without you.

My beautiful children: Thank you for making me a mom. It's truly the greatest accomplishment of my life. One day when I'm gone, I pray this book will be a roadmap for your soul. Follow the Spirit's lead; he writes the best stories.

Mom and Dad: Thank you for giving me a firm foundation of faith to stand on. Thank you for dragging me to church and forcing me to attend youth camp. It forever changed the direction of my life. And thank you for moving home. Your help, encouragement, and love are a healing balm I didn't realize I needed.

Matt and Michelle: Thank you for being my biggest cheerleaders. For real. Your words of encouragement on every blog I write, every podcast I share, and every step in the publishing process are the wind at my back. I love you.

Tom Dean: Thank you for investing your time and energy into this book. You saw potential when I doubted myself and took a chance on a mom of five from Upstate New York. What a precious gift you are in my life.

David Sluka: I'll never understand why you invested those few months to help me develop my message. I had no platform and no clue what I was doing. When I asked why, you simply said, "I prayed and feel like God wants me to do this." Thank you for being led by the Spirit. I pray his wind will carry this book farther than I ever could.

Chad Allen: Your heart for writers astounds me. You give, and give, and give, with little in return. Your reward is great in heaven, my friend. Don't ever doubt your purpose. Thank you for investing way more time than you should have in helping this book come to pass.

Jeff Braun and the Bethany House Team: Thank you for taking a shot on a nobody from nowhere who wanted to do great things for God. I love your heart for God's truth and your passion to see the gospel spread through the power of the written word. This is a dream, and I still pinch myself because I get to work with you all.

Annie F. Downs: Thank you for paving the way for Christian women authors and inspiring me to collect responses from my readers just like you did in your book *That Sounds Fun.*

New Testament Church Massena and Ogdensburg: Thank you for allowing me to be me and not forcing me to fit into the pastor's wife role. Thank you for the hours of intercession for our family and the continual support as I followed the Spirit's lead. You truly are my family.

To my prayer warriors: Thank you Barb, Elaine, and Angie for the countless hours you invested behind the scenes, interceding for the church and for our family. Every victory has your name on it.

My friends and family: Thank you for supporting my writing career. Every time you share a post, a blog, or a podcast—it matters. Not just to me, but to the lives it may touch. I wouldn't be here today without all of you holding my arms up when I was too weak to fight.

Notes

Introduction
1. David Wilkerson, John Sherrill, and Elizabeth Sherrill, *The Cross and the Switchblade: A True Story* (New York: Penguin, 1962).
2. "Our Program," Adult and Teen Challenge, September 21, 2022, https://teenchallengeusa.org/about.

Chapter 1 The White Noise of Distraction
1. Martin Luther King Jr., "I Have a Dream" (speech, Washington, DC, August 28, 1963), American Rhetoric, www.americanrhetoric.com/speeches/mlkihaveadream.htm.
2. Jason Upton, "Run Baby Run," track 4 on Jason Upton, *Dying Star*, 2002.
3. Jim Gaffigan, "Four Kids/Home Birth," YouTube video, 0:37, posted by jim gaffigan on April 16, 2020, www.youtube.com/watch?v=-Jf2IGylAhE.
4. Matthew 11:15
5. For example, Øyvind Kleiveland, "Do Sheep Only Obey Their Master's Voice?" www.youtube.com/watch?v=e45dVgWgV64.
6. Hebrews 11:6

Chapter 2 The Friction of Fear
1. Zach Dawes Jr, "Global Christian Population Projected to Reach 3.3 Billion by 2050," Good Faith Media, February 13, 2023, https://goodfaithmedia.org/global-christian-population-projected-to-reach-3-3-billion-by-2050.

Chapter 3 The Shush of Silence
1. Luke 10:38–42
2. 2 Timothy 1:9

Chapter 4 The Energy Drain

1. Judges 4:21
2. "Replantation of Digits," Mount Sinai, www.mountsinai.org/health-library /surgery/replantation-of-digits.
3. Luke 14:26
4. Matthew 10:8

Chapter 5 The Pinch of Finances

1. "How Much Money per Day Does the Average Person Live On?" Cultural World, accessed September 1, 2022, www.culturalworld.org/how-much-money -per-day-does-the-average-person-live-on.htm.
2. Genesis 14:20
3. Genesis 4:1–6
4. John 6:1–14

Chapter 6 The Pressure of Pain

1. Genesis 32:22–32
2. 1 Corinthians 15:46

Chapter 7 The Suction of Self

1. Adrian F. Ward, "The Neuroscience of Everybody's Favorite Topic," *Scientific American*, July 16, 2013, www.scientificamerican.com/article/the-neuro science-of-everybody-favorite-topic-themselves.
2. John 15:13 NLT
3. Romans 8:17
4. 2 Timothy 1:9

Chapter 8 The Comfort Zone

1. Dr. Andy Fine, "When Do You Stop Growing?," Colorado Primary Health Care, June 4, 2014, https://coloradoprimaryhealthcare.com/archives/when-do -you-stop-growing/.
2. Mariam Arain, et al, "Maturation of the Adolescent Brain," *Neuropsychiatric Disease and Treatment*, April 3, 2013, www.ncbi.nlm.nih.gov/pmc/articles /PMC3621648.
3. 2 Timothy 1:6
4. Luke 8:43–48
5. 1 Samuel 15:22

Chapter 9 The Heaviness of Hiddenness

1. John 12:24

Chapter 10 The Push to Perform

1. Matthew 3:17 NLT
2. Unknown author
3. Matthew 4:4
4. See 1 Corinthians 13:1.

Chapter 11 The Offense of Unanswered Prayer

1. Matthew 11:6
2. Craig Groeschel, *Soul Detox: Clean Living in a Contaminated World* (Grand Rapids, MI: Zondervan, 2012), 101.
3. See Ephesians 6:11–17.

Chapter 12 The Guilt Trip

1. Unknown Author
2. Exodus 17:12
3. 1 Samuel 1:1–27
4. Edward Everett Hale, "ForbesQuotes: Thoughts on the Business of Life," Forbes, www.forbes.com/quotes/author/edward-everett-hale, italics added.
5. Romans 8:19

The Legacy of the Long Game

1. "Live Life Like You Are One Hundred Years Old," YouTube video, posted by TEDx Talks on March 28, 2016, www.youtube.com/watch?v=vnatyrn6DFE.
2. Henry Ward Beecher, *Life Thoughts* (Boston: Phillips, Sampson & Co., 1858), 58.

JESSICA HURLBUT is a pastor, a writer, a runner, and a mom of five —two who struggle with autism, two adopted, and one typical teen boy who eats far too much Taco Bell.

Jessica spent nine years in the trenches of full-time ministry until 2012, when her daughter was diagnosed with level three autism. Four years later, Jessica's son was also diagnosed with severe autism. This season Jessica refers to as her *hidden years*, when God did a great and humbling work in her life. During this time, the Holy Spirit called Jessica and her husband to adopt a sibling group of two and become advocates for the 125,000 children currently in foster care who are in desperate need of a forever home.

Jesus whispered to Jessica's heart, "If you take care of my kids, I'll take care of yours."

In 2018, Jessica and Greg founded the All 4 One Adoption Day Run, in which Jessica attempted to run 110 miles in 24 hours as a visual representation of the 110,000 children in the US who were free to be adopted at that time. Since then, the adoption run has morphed into a relay where hundreds of in-person and virtual participants run five-mile legs covering a distance of 125 miles to represent the 125,000 children currently in desperate need of a forever family.

Jessica blogs at JessicaHurlbut.com, and she and her husband host a weekly podcast, *The Full Spectrum Parent*, the only faith-based autism parenting podcast in existence.

Adopt all the precious orphans. — *Sarah* Open a free counseling clinic for families and children in crisis. — *Amber* Revamp long-term elder care. — *Darcy* Support women experiencing vulnerable pregnancies and/or having children with disabilities. — *Zaly* Touch lives with his extravagant grace. — *María* Devote more time to study. — *Natalie* Feed the hungry. — *Sherry* Build a home for the elderly. — *Nicole* End the wars in the world. — *Jaqueline* Travel the world and tell everyone what Jesus did for them! — *Ally* Read the Bible all day to learn his word faster! — *Vanda* Trust him wholeheartedly, endlessly. — *Ashley* Work in overseas orphanages. — *Anastasia* Help people find freedom daily! — *Elaine* Travel to different cities preaching the gospel. — *Mandie* Overseas mission work. — *Ashley* What I do—love the homeless — *Jennifer* Stay close with Him 24/7. — *Heidi* Live out my dream. — *Alicia* Follow his teachings and share. — *Catherine* Host an annual single mothers' retreat. — *Sherley* I would bring fun abroad! — *Rachel* Better the foster-care system. — *Caroline* Produce foreign language worship albums. — *Marisa* Do full-time ministry of blogging, podcasting, and hosting conferences to spread the gospel. — *Wytinsea* Work full time in ministry. — *Raychelle* Be a mentor for other moms/young ladies. — *Miranda* Simply rest at his feet. — *Stacey* Talk people down from suicide. — *Becky* Minister to missionaries and adoptive parents. — *Jane* Give Bibles to the lost. — *Brenda* Organize nationwide Christian gatherings biannually. — *Cassidy* Change the foster-care system. — *Dorothy* Create family through coffee. — *Julie* Support sex-trafficked children. — *Martha* Tell children God loves them, no matter what! — *Heather* Adequately express my love. — *Katie* Open a home for foster kids to stay the night during an emergency situation. — *Trista* Take my children on a mission trip. — *Sarah* Adopt all the babies. — *Michelle* Spend more time with him. — *Michelle* End all human trafficking. — *Hannah* Cure autism and cancer. — *Tabitha* Give all children safe homes. — *Lydia* Open a walk-in prayer center. — *Jane* Provide basic needs for all. — *Donna Marie* Inspire hope, love, faith, and peace. — *Vanessa* Have faith in God! — *Jasmine* Raise the next generation well! — *Taína* Open a domestic violence shelter for Christian women. — *Zenna* Write Christian books and travel with family. — *Melanie* Open an after-school program for teens. — *Melanie* Bring hope to remote Alaska! — *Melody* Bring his love to everyone. — *Laurel* Write stories that move and encourage people. — *Kayla* Transform church buildings for missions. — *April* Help heal children from anything mentally, physically, etc., to become good humans. — *Jennifer* Write special-needs Bible studies. — *Jonna* Worship daily! — *Katelyn* Create stories that bring him glory. — *Alissa* Open up a rescue home. — *Christel* Live my God-given calling and pursue him with all my heart. — *Joseline* Sit with dying people. — *Lori* Write full time. — *Judith* Host people in my home every day. — *Kathy* Adopt more children. — *Jocelyn* Effectively disciple the next generation. — *Shayla* Teach my daughters to never hate, only love all people. — *Grace* Adopt every orphan. — *Angela* Build affordable homes while sharing the gospel. — *Melissa* Serve his people. — *Jenifer*

Write music and teach the Bible. —*Bethsaida*   Spend intentional time in his presence all day, every day. —*Megan*   Travel and speak to women about their hidden value. —*Nelly*   Heal people with love and kindness. —*Carmen*   Dedicate my life to missions. —*Nicole*   Help those in need get back on their feet. —*Chera*   Something that would cause my loved ones to turn to Christ! —*Kathy*   Repurpose abandoned hotels for homeless people. —*Melissa*   Share the gospel with everyone. —*Bernard*   Ministry ranch for at-risk kids. —*Susan*   Share the gospel with people! —*Julieann*   Mission work with children. —*Angie*   Evangelize. —*Alicia*   Mother all the motherless children in the world. —*Carsyn*   Help women share their stories. —*Carol*   Serve more in his name. —*Blythe*   Adopt abused and unwanted children. —*Anna*   Build a community assistance center. —*Jennifer*   Be a mother to orphans. —*Jordan*   Assist seniors, the homeless, orphans, and special-needs persons. —*Angela*   Start a school. —*Rozzie*   Adopt every homeless child. —*Vikki*   Full-time Bible college. —*Miia*   Help people know the power of redemption. —*Vidisha*   Create two books. —*Claudia*   Foster/adopt older kids. —*Jen*   Reach the lost and make disciples. —*Jen*   Build wealth with creative talents. —*Lisa*   Praise him all day long! —*Crystie*   Raise children in the way of the Lord. —*Connor*   Start an organization to help those in need and help fight human trafficking. —*Tiffani*   Open a Christian elementary school. —*Kristan*   Open up a safe space for the homeless/mentally challenged. —*Gayle*   Open a home for homeless mothers. —*Darcy*   Make quilts for widows. —*Pam*   Take care of the needy. —*Heather*   Travel and spread his love! —*Emmalee*   Make developmentally appropriate education available. —*Danielle*   Share the gospel in psychiatric wards. —*Lainey*   Start an anti-trafficking nonprofit. —*Alysse*   Make him proud of my efforts. —*Lisa*   Open a diner for lonely people. —*Minda*   Give homes to the homeless. —*Alyssa*   Foster children in need. —*Vicky*   Move overseas and care for children in orphanages. —*Tracy*   Do more for others. —*Sarah*   Expand my foster-care nonprofit. —*Sarah*   Travel the world with my husband, encouraging pastors and missionaries. Thy will be done. —*Christina*   Have several orphanages run by loving, caring Christians. —*Linette*   Help the homeless. —*Bobbi*   Counsel mothers and adopt babies! —*Jadrian*   Do nothing unless God told me to. —*Christi*   Lead more people to Christ. —*Emily*   Give him more attention. —*Colbie*   Start an orphanage. —*Tabitha*   Provide biblical healing from trauma. —*Nicole*   Break chains of mental illness. —*Amber*   Get the homeless off the streets by building a safe place for them to live and help them get back on their feet. —*Carissa*   End child and animal suffering. —*Brittney*   Care for children in Africa. —*Jennifer*   Research depression via tissue cultures. —*Briana*   Feed and help the homeless. —*Charity*   Work at an African orphanage. —*Amanda*   Bridge gap between Jesus and the elderly. —*Debbie*   Teaching homesteading sufficiency to families. —*Chanda*   Start a Jesus-centered coffee shop. —*Heather*   Permeate his love to addicts. —*Robin*   Run a health center. —*Teri*   Lead my kids to Christ. —*Crystal*   Bring Jesus into public schools. —*Bobbie*   Write children's books about Jesus. —*Rose*   Support parents in discipling kids. —*Ana*   Cook meals for people. —*Olivia*